'*Raise Resilience* is more than a parenting manual – it's a roadmap for cultivating emotionally intelligent, self-aware, and psychologically strong young people. Its strength lies in combining evidence-based practice with compassion, realness, and an accessible tone. The authors are honest about the messiness of parenting, and their vulnerability and warmth make the book especially powerful for parents navigating uncertain waters.'

Grace Lordan, *PhD, Professor in Behavioural Science, London School of Economics; author of* Think Big

'In an era where young people are overwhelmed by constant noise, disconnection, and pressure, this book is a lifeline. *Raise Resilience* is not only a roadmap for parents but a powerful invitation to help teenagers reclaim their confidence, clarity, and purpose. With wisdom rooted in science and stories that feel real, Lucy Bailey and Voula Tsoflias offer more than just advice – they offer tools to transform families and equip the next generation to thrive. Every parent, educator, and youth leader should read this.'

Karen Guggenheim, *Founder & CEO, World Happiness Summit® (WOHASU®); author of* Cultivating Happiness: Overcome Trauma and Positively Transform your Life

'This should be required reading for every parent. Combining an introduction to the brain, with good parenting, and the impact of social media, it guides parents to build resilience in their teenagers. It stands out for the wisdom of the authors and the wide range of advice. I cannot recommend it too highly.'

John Coleman, *OBE, PhD*

'This book is both a resource and a companion – for young adults, parents, and grandparents alike. It offers meaningful insights and food for thought for every stage of life.'

Eva Schwarz, *Mother, Grandmother, Harvard ALI Fellow 2023, Founder of Amity: A Preventive Loneliness Project*

Raise Resilience

This practical self-help guide introduces "Psychological Fitness" – a powerful combination of mental resilience and emotional well-being that can transform how your child navigates life's challenges. It provides brain training methods that parents and teachers can adopt and use to foster skills and knowledge in children and young people, so they can successfully navigate this uncertain and ever-changing world.

Sharing simple, proven techniques developed over two decades of successful programs with children and young people, you will find easy-to-implement tools that will help them express their worries and build their own solutions, alongside effective brain training methods that promote both mental and physical health. These will empower you to help your teenagers embrace their unique identity and develop crucial life skills. Through practical exercises, they will build a foundation of resilient thinking, emotional awareness, optimism, and empathy – essential abilities that support their well-being now and throughout adulthood.

Whether you are a parent or work with children professionally, this straightforward guide offers life-changing opportunities to support the young people in your care. The refreshingly simple techniques can be implemented right away, creating lasting positive impacts on mental and emotional health.

Lucy Bailey is chief executive officer and founder of Bounce Forward, a charity that specialises in building psychological fitness in children and the adults around them. Under Lucy's leadership the charity has reached thousands of schools, trained and supported over 30,000 teachers, and transformed the lives of over 1.2 million children and over 17,000 parents. Lucy has directed longitudinal, national research projects, is certified by University of Pennsylvania, has an MSc in practice based research, a BSc in social policy and criminology, and a post-graduate certificate in education. Recently Lucy co-authored a paper for the *Journal of the Royal Society of Medicine* looking at health education – https://bounceforward. com/wp-content/uploads/2022/12/The-poor-relation-health-eductaion-in-English-Schools-Final-.pdf.

Raise Resilience

Teach Your Teenager Well

LUCY BAILEY AND VOULA TSOFLIAS

Routledge
Taylor & Francis Group

LONDON AND NEW YORK

Designed cover image: Getty Images

First published 2026
by Routledge
4 Park Square, Milton Park, Abingdon, Oxon OX14 4RN

and by Routledge
605 Third Avenue, New York, NY 10158

Routledge is an imprint of the Taylor & Francis Group, an informa business

© 2026 Lucy Bailey and Voula Tsoflias

British Library Cataloguing-in-Publication Data
A catalogue record for this book is available from the British Library

ISBN: 978-1-032-94845-4 (hbk)
ISBN: 978-1-032-94844-7 (pbk)
ISBN: 978-1-003-58199-4 (ebk)

DOI: 10.4324/9781003581994

Typeset in Dante and Avenir
by Apex CoVantage, LLC

Access the Support Material: https://resourcecentre.routledge.com/books/9781032948447

Lucy: To Ian for our eternal love, my light: Ben and Liam.
Family is everything.

Voula: For my beloved grandchildren: Theo, Orli, Jude, Levi, Romy.

Contents

Acknowledgements

This book is inspired by the work of Bounce Forward, a UK-based charity formed in 2009 dedicated to inspiring and transforming how we think about child mental health. We nurture and build psychological fitness through the provision of evidence-based teaching tools and resources to schools, and training for parents and teachers. This work is only possible because of the people involved, who are united by passion, commitment, and thoughtful research and science, working together to build a vision of a nation where positive mental health messages help people to live mentally and emotionally well. Thank you to everyone who has walked the bridge, built the evidence, crafted the skills, and delivered the impact.

This book would not be possible without each of you, and you know who you are.

bounce forward

Introduction

We can, and should, raise our teenagers to live life to the fullest, to cherish the small moments, to savour the big pleasures, to notice the good things, to be proud of who they are, and to care about themselves and others. What better legacy could we leave them?

Happy children make happy adults.

As parents, all we want is for our precious children to grow to be physically and psychologically healthy.

The world today is increasingly complex. The pressures young people face are unique, and their parents are the first ever to raise children under the relentless spotlight of social media.

If you are one of the last generation of parents raised in an analogue world, and you have teenagers, this book is for you.

For those brave and devoted parents in the eye of the storm right now, you must rely on your own instincts. We offer you the chance to learn the skills of psychological fitness for yourselves first, and then how to teach your teenagers the same skills to help them navigate their ever-changing world. We see you as intrepid ambassadors, leading the way for future generations of parents.

DOI: 10.4324/9781003581994-1

The importance of parents

Our approach is based on a simple premise: if you want to pass on the skills of psychological fitness to teenagers, you must apply them in your own life first.

We are crucially important in supporting our youngsters to be mentally resilient, and emotionally well. One of the most powerful ways to help them learn is through our own behaviours. As we develop these skills ourselves, we become effective role models, demonstrating how to think clearly and behave effectively.

The way we respond as parents is a vital opportunity to build helpful and healthy connections in the brains of our children.

Imagine this

Hannah, aged twelve, had been invited to join a community art club. She didn't know anyone and had become a little anxious about walking through the door on the first night. Her mum, worried by her daughter's anxiety, talked a lot, bombarding Hannah with questions about how she was feeling and what she was worried about. That intensified Hannah's worries so much so that she decided she didn't want to go. Her mum felt relieved and told Hannah they could do art together, in the comfort of their own home.

Amelia, also twelve, had been invited to join a community art club. She didn't know anyone and had become a little anxious about walking through the door on the first night. Her mum recognised that her anxiety was normal; she wasn't that good at meeting new people either. She asked Amelia about what she loved about art and drawing, and how it made her feel when she was being creative. She told her she was proud of her for taking up such a great hobby and admitted that she too could be nervous. Then she explained to Amelia what she did just before meeting people for the first time: she took some long deep breaths in and out, as she counted to ten to settle herself down; then she told herself you can do this, you won't be the only person that is new, you'll make some great new friends, the pain is worth the gain. Amelia agreed that that might be helpful, and she would give it a try. They decided to go for a pizza after the club as a celebration.

These are two different ways of establishing the connections and patterns in Hannah and Amelia's brains. One has the potential to develop a new way of thinking about meeting new people, offering a positive learning experience, and most importantly, the result of Amelia benefiting from the social experience at the new club. The other means Hannah had given up and is less likely to try new things in future. Her mother had confirmed: doing new things is frightening and best avoided.

What is psychological fitness?

Psychological fitness is a combination of mental resilience and emotional well-being, skills that are essential for the growth and development of today's teenagers. Our goal is to guide, support, and encourage you, as you face this unique set of circumstances. Experience has shown us that with practice, psychological fitness can be taught and mastered for enhanced happiness, well-being, and life skills.

Mental resilience is having the ability to:

- Think flexibly and be adaptable to different situations.
- Connect and communicate with others and reach out for support when needed.
- Learn from setbacks, uncertainty, and failures.
- Keep things in perspective and not catastrophise.
- Have self-confidence that is grounded in reality.

Emotional well-being is having the ability to:

- Understand, regulate, and express emotions.
- Control and understand impulses to act unhelpfully.
- Have empathy and compassion for self and others.
- Take action to recover and replenish energy.

Children's circumstances and biology vary widely, so having a tool kit of practical skills that can be used in different ways means they are equipped with the psychological fitness that works best in the context of their reality.

Our approach combines well-founded theoretical concepts from years of sound research with our understanding of how to build mental resilience and emotional well-being in young people. The research is an important base, but how to apply the learning practically is what this book is about. We have learned, taught, and practised these skills for decades, through our work in schools training teachers and parents, in leadership programmes for the corporate world, and, vitally, we have applied the learning personally to ourselves and our children.

Learning the skills

The skills will be presented in a series of chapters that each focus on one of the skills of psychological fitness, set out in a specific sequence. The skills combine and build on each other, intensifying the power of each element to create a kind of collective magic, so it's important to learn the skills from start to finish.

We encourage you to read the chapters in sequence, thoughtfully, slowly, reflectively, so that you can fully engage with the exercises and activities. The material is rich, so take your time, don't try and take it in all at once. Concentrate on each chapter and deepen your reading and understanding by completing the worksheets. Once you have completed a full read through, you might wish to enhance and refresh your learning by picking and choosing the chapters that have been particularly striking or relevant to you.

Building practical skills is a distinct discipline. Think of learning to drive a car – the lesson separates the component parts: starting the engine; steering the wheel; changing gears; learning to brake. Each function is learned in isolation, and, crucially, **practised repeatedly,** so that the learning becomes a skill that is almost automatic. It is only after each function has been learned in this way that it all comes together with grace and ease, and you are finally skilled at driving the car. Practice makes perfect. With repetition, the component parts of psychological fitness become so much a part of your everyday life that you don't see it as a separate function or skill, it simply becomes part of who you are.

The skills of psychological fitness develop as building blocks, starting with understanding ourselves and our emotions. The following graphic shows the developmental nature of the different elements in sequence.

The four skills of self-awareness show us how to respond and recognise when our reactions become obstructions. These provide a strong foundation from which we can challenge and change the way we think and behave, and not only when dealing with setbacks and difficulties. We will learn to take control and feel clear and confident in the decisions we make.

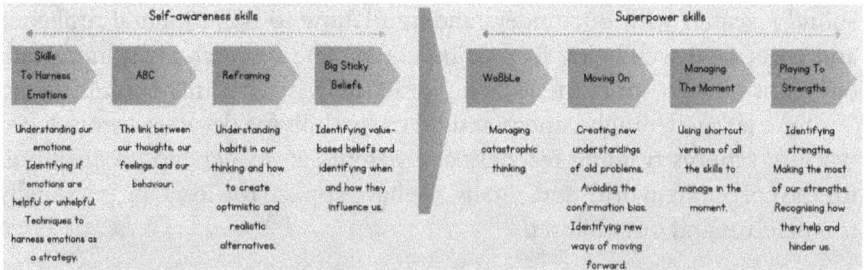

Self-awareness skills				Superpower skills			
Skills To Harness Emotions	ABC	Reframing	Big Sticky Beliefs	WeBbLe	Moving On	Managing The Moment	Playing To Strengths
Understanding our emotions. Identifying if emotions are helpful or unhelpful. Techniques to harness emotions as a strategy.	The link between our thoughts, our feelings, and our behaviour.	Understanding habits in our thinking and how to create optimistic and realistic alternatives.	Identifying value-based beliefs and identifying when and how they influence us.	Managing catastrophic thinking.	Creating new understandings of old problems. Avoiding the confirmation bias. Identifying new ways of moving forward.	Using shortcut versions of all the skills to manage in the moment.	Identifying strengths. Making the most of our strengths. Recognising how they help and hinder us.

The four superpower skills deepen our understanding and allow us to be the best version of ourselves, living life in all its richness, with hope, optimism, and vigour, to influence and enable the changes we want to see for ourselves and our families.

Each chapter begins with a description of the skill and how it helps from a scientific perspective. Then a case study illustrates how this would look, sound, and feel in situations that we can all regularly face. Our series of case studies focus on our imaginary family, who we will follow as they face their everyday lives together. Families come in all shapes and sizes, in many forms and with many differences. We have chosen our example family thoughtfully, to keep the focus on the skills of psychological fitness, which is the same for all families, regardless of any differences.

Exercises and activities will give you a feel for how the skill works, along with some top tips to help you use the techniques for yourself first. This is your opportunity to *practise*, repeatedly, for the skill to become part of you. You may find it useful to keep a notebook or journal to hand. Each chapter will close with ideas for you to try with your teenagers.

Our aim is to empower you, as a parent, to provide your teenagers with proven techniques to be healthy in mind and body, and a structured language framework to help you support them. You will learn how to help them express their worries and their concerns, and how to build their own unique solutions to challenges.

These practical thinking and emotional skills can be used throughout life, for you and your family, passing them on for lifelong personal growth across many generations.

Why psychological fitness is needed now more than ever

Fifty percent of lifelong mental ill health problems start by the age of fourteen.[1]

That is a truly shocking statistic, but so are global pandemics, political turmoil, war, and the speed of information technology. It's an intense pace of change to keep up with, emphasising the urgent need for all teenagers to be taught these skills at school and at home.

Being a teenager has never been more challenging, and adolescence is a crucial developmental turning point, providing a particularly receptive time to learn this practical method.

We want our adolescent children to be physically and psychologically fit. That is achieved by making the deliberate effort to cultivate regular habits of thought, emotion, and behaviour that will lead to enhanced personal development. Parents, and other adults, play a crucial role in this, by the way we talk, listen, guide, and support them. We can make a profound difference to the speed and pace of learning for our next generation.

> *When it comes to mental health, prevention is better than cure, and education is better than prevention.*

During physical education, our teenagers learn about activities that keep them fit, strong, and healthy. It's the same with psychological education: a positive approach to living well, rather than a response to mental illness.

Bringing the expertise to life in the real world

> *Adults' response and support for their youngsters is vital to their future development.*

It is one thing to understand the concept of a skill, but the ideas only become useful when we can apply them in our real lives. We will guide you towards this, as we encounter the imaginary family of Carla and Pete, and their children Joe, aged fourteen, Ella, eleven, and Lilly, eight, and through practical activities that will help both you and your teenager.

We are Lucy and Voula and our expertise comes not only through years of experience working with parents, teachers, professionals, and young people, but also because we are real people who have walked the walk of applying the skills as we encountered the rich and rocky road of our lives so far.

Lucy

I'm a mum of two, Nana of one, aunty, sister, daughter, friend, and, I'm told, a respected authority on well-being, as an expert in the field for more than twenty years. My passion for enabling others to overcome setbacks and to pursue opportunity started when I sat in a conference listening to a head teacher who explained that at his school they taught responsibility and how to fail well. It was a light bulb moment for me: if only I had been taught that failure was a learning opportunity, I would have been an A star student at it! I have lived experience of leaving school too early with limited qualifications, overcoming a violent relationship, and facing breast cancer when my children were just two and five. I am a carer for my disabled mother and currently supporting my husband with incurable cancer. Life can be tough, but my passion is to drive a movement to influence a positive change with psychological fitness at the core.

What Voula says about Lucy is how passionate she is to change the education system, making personal sacrifices for the sake of her charity. She's a force of nature, an inspiration, on a mission to ensure that every teenager receives an education in psychological fitness throughout secondary school, as a standard part of the school syllabus. I would love to be part of making that happen.

Voula

I'm an author, psychologist, charity trustee, and, most importantly, mother of five adult children and stepchildren, and devoted Nana to five grandchildren aged one to six. So I have plenty of experience in raising resilient young people. I was born in South Wales, in a Greek clan. Life was very challenging in many ways; it would have been so much smoother for me if I had learned the skills of psychological fitness as a teenager. It is said that a person's happiness in life is determined by how happy they are at the age of sixteen. I almost died when I was that age, after falling through a glass door in a rage. Learning and teaching the skills in our book as an adult has profoundly changed me. Since retiring from my career as a chartered psychologist working with business leaders, I've concentrated on my lifelong passion for writing. As well as four novels, I was one of the authors of *The Psychology Book*, which won the book of the year award in 2012. I've loved being involved in shaping Bounce Forward for the last seventeen years; I'm totally committed to the cause.

What Lucy says about Voula is how she is simply the powerhouse at the heart of her very large and extended family. She is extraordinary in her capability to be what others need in troubling times. A shoulder to cry on, the voice of reason, a planner, confidante, carer, supporter, and coach, and often to different people at the same time. Voula radiates empathy and I am forever grateful to be writing this book alongside her.

Note

1   Kessler RC, Berglund P, Demler O, Jin R, Merikangas KR, Walters EE. (2005). Lifetime Prevalence and Age-of-Onset Distributions of DSM-IV Disorders in the National Comorbidity Survey Replication. *Archives of General Psychiatry*, 62(6), 593–602. https://doi.org/10.1001/archpsyc.62.6.593

Being a child is different now   1

Teaching your teenagers well

Our world has changed dramatically in the last fifty years, and our children's experience of growing up is different to any previous generation. That is a lot for parents to come to grips with. Each new generation experiences a new and evolved understanding of the world, as specific events shape our lives.

One of the hardest things about being a parent of a teenager is the recognition that their world is very different to the one we grew up in, and so our experience, while useful to some degree, is probably mostly unhelpful. So how do we best guide them?

Human connection, sleep, and social media are interrelated in complex ways that impact the mental health of our teenagers.

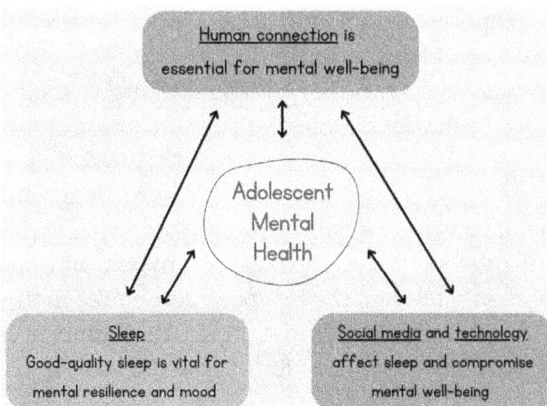

DOI: 10.4324/9781003581994-2

Human connection matters

As technology becomes more efficient, human contact decreases.

We are social beings, primed to feel better together. When we connect socially there is a decrease in the body's stress response; when we help others, it leaves us feeling less anxious and more secure. Cavemen survived, not because they were brave or strong or smarter than the other creatures, but because of their strength in groups.

Our desire for connection is evident in three-month-old babies, who favour familiar faces. They become attuned to signals from those closest to them, their bodily cues, tone of voice, patterns of speech, and facial recognition. Early babyhood is the period when attachments are laid down, a crucial time for the development of trust and safety.

Even the most sophisticated Artificial Intelligence cannot match this intricate signalling.[1] That's why technological social networking is an inferior substitute for face-to-face interpersonal communication.

Human connection matters more now than ever before.

- People with strong social connections live longer; in fact, they are fifty percent less likely to die prematurely than people with weak connections.[2]
- Social networks erode our time in human contact, including religious participation, community membership, and the frequency with which we invite friends over.[3]
- Advances in transportation mean loved ones live further away.
- We enjoy the convenience of home delivery. Amazon and the internet have changed our shopping habits. There's no need to leave the house or interact with anyone.
- University campuses are quieter places, where many lectures happen online for students sitting alone in their rooms.
- Bars and restaurants are full of people looking at their phones rather than talking to each other.

Social media can be a good place to connect with friends and share stories and pictures, but it can leave us feeling inadequate when we see the stunning achievements of others, with many likes, comments, and shares.

Just as we, and our children, should spend some time in the fresh air daily, we should also spend some time in close physical proximity to another human being. This is particularly important for the mental health of young people.

So, the world our teenagers are growing into as adults is a very different place. Our role as parents must adapt and change to help and support them to develop their resilience, shape their hope and optimism, and make changes that are in their best interests.

> *After all they are the leaders of the future and the parents of the next generation.*

The power of sleep

There are some simple yet crucial things we can all do to foster the mental health of our teenagers on a habitual basis. Doing something once changes nothing. Doing something frequently and regularly builds over time to make big changes. Sleeping well is at the top of the list:

- Good sleep
- Human connection
- Physical exercise
- Limit your screen time
- Time spent outdoors daily

Sleep is essential because it plays a vital role in physical and mental development. During sleep our brains are as active as during the day[4]. The stereotype of teenagers who stay up late and wake up late is all too accurate: melatonin, which makes us sleepy, is released later at night in many teenagers, so it's harder for them to sleep, and then they wake up late.

> *For young people it's a time when growth hormones are released, and memories are consolidated.*

During deep sleep, our glymphatic system, sometimes called the rinse programme, repairs and cleans our brains of toxic substances, to support our mental health. Sleep also helps regulate emotions: we are far more likely to feel down and irritable when we are tired.

Good healthy sleep can be disturbed by noise, worries of every kind, late release of melatonin, and too much time on social media. Chronic sleeplessness is positively dangerous to our mental and physical health, so finding ways to maintain good sleep habits is essential.

The information technology revolution

The ways in which we communicate and relate to each other have been transformed, starting with the advent of radio and television and later with computing, the internet, broadband, and, more recently, mobile phones and tablets. Each new advance has seen our access to information grow, starting with images in newspapers, developing to television screens, and now in the palms of our hands. The difference between reading about a war, a riot, or a plane crash to seeing it evolve on a screen shows us vividly the scale of change.

People born after 1997 do not remember a world without the internet. They use their mobile devices and digital platforms to learn, play, and socialise. This hyperconnectivity is independent and distinct from any generation that came before. Digital technology has advanced faster than parents have been able to keep pace with. There is some evidence that, for children, one or two hours a day of screen time is probably OK, but much more than that may be detrimental. We just don't know. Yet parents must make decisions that have never ever had to be faced before. For example, when should my child:

- Have a mobile phone, if ever?
- Be connected to the internet?
- Be able to use a computer unsupervised?

By around 2008, the world had fast broadband available in the home, Facebook was born, and so was the smartphone. It was a perfect storm. The current generation who are parenting teenagers were the last to live in an analogue world. Now, for their own children, they must make up the rules as they go along. They cannot rely on past experience of their own, or from guidance from their own parents.

Eventually, research and history will tell its own story, but for those brave and devoted parents in the eye of the storm, they must rely on their own instincts.

> *We do not yet fully understand the impact that our ever-growing relationship with technology is having on our children.*

Today's parents are far more aware of the dangers among us than their own parents were. New laws have been created to protect children and keep them safe, in a way that a child born during the Second World War wouldn't have experienced. We listen to the views, needs, and wants of our children like never before and we supervise them frequently, watching their every move, perhaps hoping to catch them before they fall.

Through social media our teenagers are used to having their every move recorded, shared, discussed, and critiqued. Of course, our children need to be connected; it's part of everyday life now, but it shouldn't be a full-time activity.

We do need to keep lines of communication open with our youngsters and we can do that by being honest and talking to them on a certain level, as you might with another adult. Technology is all around us and we will be engaging with and being influenced by the latest trends ourselves.

As parents we need to engage with our teenagers about the real world around them, to have conversations with them in a curious and open way. One way to do this is to show them how we are thinking about our own influences and behaviour. Is our phone ever present? Do we ignore them while we are engrossed in our social media timeline? Talk to them on a level, adult to adult, about the advantages and disadvantages of technologies and social media in an open and flexible way. After all there are two sides to most situations. Reflect on the ways we have been, and still are, influenced by the messages we receive, and how they have changed over time. For example, think about old versus new adverts and the differences: now we are bombarded with adverts based on our previous search history online, and how intrusive this can be compared to seeing a billboard advertisement out on the street.

Parents of children today are leading the way. We do not fully understand the impact technology is having. It's not all bad, there are many transformational advances, but we do need to press pause when it comes to our teenagers, especially regarding social media.

Today's generation of adolescents are sometimes called Gen Alphas. They are the children born between 2010–2025, so the eldest is fifteen years old. They are the first generation born into a digital world where remote classrooms, smartphones, tablets and streaming are all commonplace from an early age.

They are characterised like this:

- **Hyperconnected.** They are permanently connected with current and emerging technologies as an integral way of life.
- **Independent.** They are influenced from beyond the family unit and can form their own opinions, and they expect their individual needs and preferences to be considered.
- **Visuals.** Moving images, short reels, bitesize videos are their preferred formats. Digital games will boost their visual skills, improving hand–eye coordination and the ability to easily switch tasks.

- **Technological.** Having grown up being hyper-connected, they will be experts in the use of new technologies. They have an intrinsic capacity for learning, meaning the possibilities for expanding digital development are vast.
- **Diverse.** They will be diverse in their lifestyle choices, what they like and dislike. They will accept different points of view, be comfortable with varied ethnicities, more travelled, with broad work experiences as they move from job to job.

And they face some distinct challenges:

- **Reduced attention span and concentration.** As they are used to quick, impactful bite-sized information, their attention span is reduced, and their concentration is impaired.
- **Less time for socialising.** Captivated by a digital world, they do not value or see the need for learning, playing, and socialising in more traditional ways. In fact, much of their socialisation is transferred to social networks.
- **Less development of creativity and imagination.** With growing reliance on technology and Artificial Intelligence for creativity and imagination, development in these areas will suffer.
- **Reduced ability to achieve happiness.** Lack of sleep due to the use of social media will continue to evaporate a sense of worth, increase loneliness, and drive anxiety.

> *There is a link between the rise of smartphones and social media and the increase in depression, anxiety, and loneliness in today's youth.*[5]

Today's parents cannot rely on past experience, their own, or their parents', to make decisions about what is in the best interest of children growing up in this new world. That's tough, when we don't know the true impact that the constantly changing technology is having.

We urge you to be bold and brave in your decisions about how your children engage with technology. Creating some family guidelines about how, when, and why to engage with social media can be super helpful. Here are some examples you could include:

- Limit the time spent on social platforms. Connect more with people face to face.
- Take a break from online games and electronic devices particularly in the lead-up to bedtime.

- Use social platforms to connect with others to spread kindness or to learn new things.
- Don't connect with people who cause negative drama for you or the people / things you care about.
- From time to time reflect on the amount of fun versus angst you feel when engaging with social media.
- If you think something might be offensive or inappropriate, don't share it.
- Don't be pressured to share or do something online that you know is not right.
- Do not do anything online that you would not be happy sharing with close family members, a future boss, the police.
- Don't believe the first thing you find online; find different and varied sources for information.
- Know where to find help and support with concerns online.

As parents our relationship with technology matters, because we are role models. Our young people will copy us from their early years, noticing how we have our phones with us constantly. An entire range of toy mobile phones and tablets exist so that they can be just like Mummy and Daddy. Be thoughtful about the behaviour you are modelling to them.

Parents can usefully ask themselves some questions:

- Do I prioritise my phone over other forms of contact?
- How much of my time on social media am I enjoying?
- Am I spending lots of time refreshing screens for validation?
- Can I go without my phone and have fun?
- Am I spending more time online than I am in the company of others?
- Do I think about the implications of posting about my children?
- Do I use technology to keep my child quiet because I am busy?
- Am I aware of when, how, and why my teenager is using technology including social platforms?

Unhappy teenagers

Mental ill health has a devastating impact on children's lives.[6]

The state of child mental ill health today is depressing and accurate in equal measure. The western world is full of news stories that paint a miserable picture of unhappy young people against a backdrop of unlimited opportunities that on the face of it should mean their happiness is rising, not dropping. Whether teenagers are less happy now than they were in say the 1960s, when life was perceived as simpler, more innocent, is a debate for a different book. What we can say is that we notice how children seem to feel their emotions more today, expressing how they feel about things as part of everyday conversation.

Having an unhappy child at home is an unbearably difficult experience, and often hardest as the teenage years approach. Knowing how to respond to their moods, tears, and tantrums is complicated. Most of us will remember that moment in the supermarket when our three-year-old threw themselves to the ground, screaming and crying because they couldn't have sweeties. We even laughed about it with friends and family later, but somehow the same is not so true for dealing with teenage tantrums. Our fourteen-year-olds should know better, and if they don't then the finger of blame is directed firmly at parents. We are letting them get away with it, or we are too soft, or a helicopter parent, or too involved, or too weak. These thoughts mean sharing tales of teenager challenges with each other in a more complicated, more nuanced way. Sometimes it's easier to bury and ignore that, at least for now. It's just too hard.

We know that our brains are not fully formed until our mid to late twenties. Being a teenager is confusing and there is a lot to learn. The adolescent brain is exposed to a torrent of influences, mostly through social media: body image, pornography, chilling global issues such as war, climate change, falling out of love, fitting in. No wonder that teenagers react badly and no wonder it's easier to avoid what's really happening. Life is complex, and teenagers are getting to grips with the messy twentieth century world during the second most influential brain development period of their life, after the first twelve months.

Fortunately, the ideas for raising psychologically fit children are refreshingly simple and easy to implement.

Yet they will deliver life-changing opportunities to connect in ways that are helpful to parents, and other adults around teenagers.

The way adults behave and respond matters. Our attempts to make things ok, to try and rationalise their sadness away, can cause teenagers to retreat, to stop talking or trying to explain, in their efforts to untangle the mess inside their head.

When the skills of psychological fitness are developed, children and the adults around them function better and feel good in their everyday lives.

When it comes to mental health, prevention is better than cure, and education is better than prevention.

Summary

Children's experience of growing up today is different from any previous generation. Adolescent mental health is impacted by the transformation of our lives brought about by information technology. Today's parents need to think on their feet about what is in the best interest of children growing up in this new world. We have learnt that:

- Human connection, sleep, and social media are interrelated in complex ways that impact the mental health of our teenagers.
- The technology industry is growing faster than we can understand the impact it is having on our children's development.
- Parents today are leading the way as they navigate the digital revolution and make decisions about the behaviour they model and set boundaries for the way their children interact with social media.
- When it comes to the mental health of our children, prevention is better than cure, and education is better than prevention.
- Teaching the skills of psychological fitness can deliver life-changing opportunities to connect in ways that are helpful to parents, and other adults around teenagers.

Notes

1   Smith A, Phoenix van Wagoner H, Keplinger K, Celebi C. (2025). Navigating AI Convergence in Human – Artificial Intelligence Teams: A Signaling Theory Approach. *Journal of Organisational Behaviour.* https://doi.org/10.1002/job.2856

2   Holt-Lunstad J, Smith TB, Layton JB. (2010). Social Relationships and Mortality Risk: A Meta-Analytic Review. *PLOS Medicine,* 7(7), e1000316. https://doi.org/10.1371/journal.pmed.1000316

3   Clark A. (2007). *Understanding Community: A Review of Networks, Ties and Contacts ESRC National Centre for Research Methods.* NCRM Working Paper Series 9/07. https://eprints.ncrm.ac.uk/id/eprint/469/1/0907_understanding_community.pdf

4   Coleman J. (2021). *The Teacher and the Teenage Brain.* Routledge.

5   Abi-Jaoude E, Naylor KT, Pignatiello A. (2020, February 10). Smartphones, Social Media Use and Youth Mental Health. *Canadian Medical Association Journal,* 192(6), E136–E141. https://doi.org/10.1503/cmaj.190434. PMID: 32041697; PMCID: PMC7012622.

6   The Good Childhood Report 2024. Retrieved April 2025. www.childrenssociety.org.uk/information/professionals/resources/good-childhood-report-2024

Our amazing brains 2

The human brain is truly remarkable: each one is composed of billions of cells called neurons. Inside our individual heads there are more of them than all the stars in the galaxy. They are all connected in some way. Even with the huge advances in scanning technology, there is still a great deal to understand about how this network operates. There are often disputes between experts about the precise functions of the various areas of the brain.

> *As our children grow, particularly through adolescence, major brain changes are happening.*[1]

Alongside that, our teenagers are moving through puberty and adjusting to physical and psychological changes. It helps us to recognise that the way our children react to things is part of their growth, and while it might feel unsettling, we can learn how to help them through it.

The brain is our engine room, a complicated machine that controls every aspect of our thoughts, feelings, and actions. As parents, it's helpful to have a basic understanding to help us in our conversations with our teenagers. So, let's take a look at some key brain parts that will help us understand them.

The prefrontal cortex (PFC)

This is the surface of the brain. It is involved in many important functions, such as problem-solving, staying focused, decision-making, thinking clearly, and controlling the urge to react. The PFC uses information from both

DOI: 10.4324/9781003581994-3

the outside world and various parts of the brain to generate a response to matters as they arise. For example, helping us to stay focused and concentrate so we can take a penalty kick at goal, helping to work out a riddle, or find a way out of a maze, showing our personality, and regulating our social behaviour so as not to embarrass ourselves. In a nutshell, it organises our thoughts and actions.

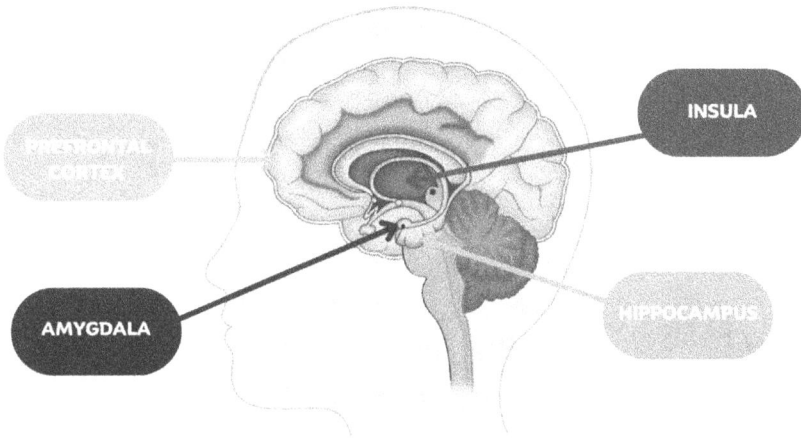

The limbic system

This is a group of brain structures that control our emotions, drive our actions, and impact our behaviour, learning, and memory. It's a bridge between the mind and body. Organs include the amygdala, the hippocampus, and the insula.

The **amygdala** is a tiny organ that is the emotional centre of the brain, responsible for alerting us to danger and preparing us to act: we might fight to confront the danger; or flee, run away; or we might play dead, by freezing or fainting; or we could fawn, seeking out someone powerful to protect us. Over our lifetime, and especially during our younger years, our amygdala creates a database of difficult and dangerous experiences, to help us avoid similar situations in the future. This is how we learn what is dangerous, a vital means of our survival as a species. One drawback of this is that our amygdala may overgeneralise and categorise some experiences as dangerous when they are not. But we might react as though they are.

Neural activity in the limbic system regulates our centres of excitation and soothing. Studies on young babies showed that centres of excitation were activated in the presence of the father, and the centres of soothing were activated by the mother. Intriguingly, this effect appeared in response to photographs of the parents, as well as their presence. This neural activity is generally outside our conscious awareness. As we develop, we learn to balance our needs for excitement and soothing, and, if we are aware of that balance, we can manage our emotions more effectively.

The **hippocampus** is where learning and memories are stored. Short-term memories are organised and transferred to our long-term memory bank, helping us with decision-making, communication, and much more. The hippocampus produces a fresh supply of neurons which is vital for learning because this helps to override the amygdala response by remembering how to deal with a difficult situation or to recognise it wasn't that bad after all.

The **insula**, deep inside the brain, is the area that reads the physical state of the entire body, generating urges that drive actions, such as eating, feeling guilty, or reacting emotionally to a song.

Happy healthy teenagers

> *All parents want their teenagers to be healthy and happy, and the two are intertwined.*

Healthy children are usually happier, and happier children are usually healthier. The key to good health is learning skills that equip us to make healthy choices. There is no doubt that education is a key factor of health. School is also important, though academic learning is only half the story. We are social and emotional creatures and so the strength of those skills is just as important, and in the best interests of humanity. If we are to live well, and have empathy for others, we must nurture our teenagers' social and emotional skills, which have a direct link to health and happiness throughout our lives.

Ages and stages for building psychological fitness

Resilience matters throughout our lives, building and growing as our experiences teach us to understand ourselves in the context of an ever-changing world. Life will never be the same after meeting a life partner, the passing of someone close, diagnosis of incurable ill health, natural disasters. These are major turning points that shape what we believe to be true, how we see the world, and how we respond to it.

We can help our teenagers to learn the skills that will support them in the development of their psychological fitness. As well as the intellectual learning of how it all works, you will learn how to apply the skill in your everyday life. What works for one person won't necessarily be useful for another. That is the wonder of the skills; how we use them will vary from person to person, moment to moment, and situation to situation. You will make the skill your own, so much so that you no longer think of it as a skill, but just the way you respond and deal with the world and the situations in front of you.

There are different ways to build psychological resilience, depending on the age and development stage of our children.

Babyhood

During the early months and years of infancy, the levels of mental resilience and emotional well-being in the adults caring for babies is crucial to their development. Babies' brains are developing in fundamental ways that will impact them for life. Looking after ourselves is how we create a stable safe environment for them, so we will be better placed to respond to their needs. Everything we do with our babies is offering the potential to spark healthy brain development. When we feel good and can function well in ourselves, we are more able to talk to them, relax and enjoy them, cuddle, and play with them: the building blocks for healthy brains.

Children

Children from three to eight years old are like sponges, watching and mimicking what they see around them. They are picking up clues and cues from the adults close to them. This is the perfect stage for modelling resilience, letting them see us fail and come out the other side, to celebrate the effort it took to achieve our successes. This is when to provide opportunities for them to experiment, safely of course, to experience other children and adults so they develop essential social skills. We can praise their responses to disappointment, how they stuck with it, came through it, how they tried different things, and didn't give up, or how they played with another child with kindness.

Adolescence

This is a prime time to teach new skills. Teenagers are still prepared to learn from us, despite what they might say. If we can get this right, they will continue to learn from us. Between the ages of nine to thirteen, sometimes called the tweenage years, is the opportunity for them to learn about mental resilience and emotional well-being both at school and at home. Then our children can explore the skills in different contexts and environments, learning with their peers, because sometimes teenagers can be less inclined to listen to their parents. There are good brain developmental reasons why this happens; they are after all moving towards adulthood. At this time, they will want and need to listen to those outside the family unit, other adults, and older peers. They are starting to develop their own sense of self and become more independent. Parents can still teach skills that enable them to understand themselves and in doing so create understanding and compassion for others.

Young adults

For our young adults, at fourteen and up, the way we communicate is crucial. What we talk about, and how we listen and to respond to them, is key to their development. Sometimes though, this can be uncomfortable if we don't like what we hear, and we'd really rather not know what's going on for them. Staying calm, non-judgemental, and really listening with empathy to their experience will keep lines of communication open, and the door ajar to keep guiding them. Having the ability to listen to them without necessarily having all the answers is a great skill: we can simply be glad that they told us. We can ask: how can I help? and prepare ourselves for when they say: you can't. At this age they need to work things out for themselves, knowing you are there. Caring and being a safety net if they fall is the best way of nurturing their resilience.

Neurodiversity

The brain is truly remarkable and yet the narrative around mental health remains disproportionately influenced by mental *ill* health, that is, understanding the brain when it is unwell, diseased, disabled. Conditions such as Attention Deficit Hyperactivity Disorder (ADHD) highlight the prevailing focus on what is missing compared to people *without* ADHD. Special Educational Needs, or SEN, is a deficit term widely used in schools to highlight children for what they are deemed to lack, when we know that children learn in different ways. Neurodiversity is a term that looks at brain functioning and behaviour as a normal variation rather than a disorder.[2]

We love this strength-based approach to brain diversity, with its focus on inclusion, enriched lives, and the development of potential. We are all wonderfully diverse and each brain works differently, and unique qualities should be recognised as a strength.

Coming at differences with this positive standpoint means one's sense of self is developed in a healthy way. We can use language that creates opportunity for what we want to see rather than what we don't. For example:

- Walk on the path, rather than don't run on the road.
- The kind part of what you said there was . . . and I felt so proud of you.
- It took courage and strength to calm down and walk away.

Minor changes in the way we talk to our teenagers can make all the difference in them behaving in the way we would like to see, as opposed to constant nagging and arguing about what we don't what to see. "You need to explain yourself right now" is more likely to end up in an argument compared with "I want to understand it from your side, so let's take a ten-minute break so we can talk calmly with each other."

If we only think of differences from a deficit angle, that is, what is my child lacking? rather than how a unique superpower could be an advantage, we are blocking development. Each person and certainly every teenager deserves to feel empowered and appreciated for who they are, because their perspective and way of seeing the world is of value. It is in this vein that we explore the skills we will cover, all of which are useful to varying degrees for everyone.

Summary

The brain is a deeply complex organ. Having some basic understanding is useful for parents. We have learnt that:

- The brain is the engine room for our thoughts, feelings, and behaviours.
- There are different ways to build resilience depending on the age of our children.
- The teenage years are the second most impactful time for our brains. There is a huge amount of activity, development, learning, and laying down helpful or unhelpful neural pathways.
- Our brains are unique and different; that is what makes us wonderfully distinctive.

Activities for teenagers

At the end of each chapter, we will offer some activities to try with your teenage children, some of which are useful for younger children too. Be thoughtful about when to introduce them. You know your children best, so you decide what, when, and how to share the ideas. Make it an authentic learning moment, the same way you might teach your child anything. Maybe you could explain that you have been reading this book and that it is helping you think and learn about yourself.

What is resilience?

This activity aims to help your teenager think about what resilience is. It is useful to begin by explaining that setbacks and challenges are a part of life; maybe you could talk about a time when you or someone close to you had to overcome a setback. Keep it a small everyday type of example but bring to life the idea that we must build our resilience so that we are able to cope and survive difficult times, and that resilience can also help us to be at our best. You might tell them that you have been learning about resilience for yourself, and that you have been able to see how it is something that is helpful throughout life.

Choose one of the following options for them to depict what being resilient means to them:

- Create a photo collage of pictures from magazine or brochure cutouts.
- Draw a picture using art equipment you have at home.
- Use recycling, cardboard, and garden waste.
- Sit and talk and share ideas together.

As well as getting creative, think about ways you are already resilient.

As part of this activity make sure they understand that whilst resilience is lots of different things, it has also been studied over many years. Next is a summary of what the research tells us about resilience for you to compare with the lists created at home.

Resilience is being able to:

- Understand, regulate, and express emotions.
- Control our impulses before we act.
- Learn from setbacks, uncertainty, and failures.

- Think flexibly and adapt to different situations.
- Keep things in perspective and don't catastrophise.
- Connect with others and reach out for support when needed.
- Have empathy and compassion for self and others.
- Have self-confidence that is grounded in reality.

Famous failures

Research and create a quiz about well-known successful people that failed along the way to success. Include at least some people your children and family will recognize; do also include some less well known. The quiz winner could share a "failure" that they have had to overcome, and what they did.

Here are some ideas with answers to start off with.

- What is the name of the movie, made by George Lucas, that was rejected by every movie studio in Hollywood? **STAR WARS**
- WD40 is a famous brand for different oils, lubricants. Why does it include "40" in its name? **IT TOOK THIRY-NINE FAILED ATTEMPTS TO DESIGN THE FINAL SUCCESSFUL PRODUCT**
- Who, after several failed music acts nearly went bankrupt in 1989, went on to create a record label and a series of reality-based singing and talent shows? **SIMON COWELL**
- Who, at age seven, was kicked out of school for asking too many questions? He had poor hearing, and a teacher told him he was too stupid to learn anything. He went on to light up the world! **THOMAS EDISON, INVENTED THE LIGHT BULB**
- Who was the single unemployed mother, who picked up a pen and paper and became a leading author? Many films were made based on her books. **JK ROWLING**
- Who was fired from the company he created, only to be rehired and go on to create some of the greatest technologies such as the iPad, iPhone, MacBook? **STEVE JOBS**
- Who was rejected by every vacuum manufacturer, and had over 5,000 failed designs before going on to develop a very well-known vacuum brand? **JAMES DYSON**
- Who was told he lacked creativity and was fired from a newspaper because he had no original ideas? He went on to start, arguably, the most famous movie company. **WALT DISNEY**

Notes

1 Coleman J. (2021). *The Teacher and the Teenage Brain*. Routledge.
2 Baumer N. (2021). *What Is Neurodiversity: Mind and Mood*. Harvard Health Publishing, Harvard Medical School. Retrieved April 2025. www.health. harvard.edu/blog/what-is-neurodiversity-202111232645

The art of self-regulation 3
Using our emotions strategically

The pursuit of happiness, of human well-being, inspired groundbreaking research in positive psychology. This is the scientific study of the brain when it's working at its best, a counterpoint for the mass of research that, historically, has studied what's gone wrong when the brain is ill, depressed, or psychotic. This new focus is interested in the role of positive emotions, the power of thinking optimistically, identifying strengths, and of living a psychologically rich life.

There are different ways for us to understand how we are doing in terms of our levels of well-being. How satisfied we are is based on whether we feel our lives are worthwhile or not. Are we hopeful for the future? Does the world treat us fairly? The way we answer these questions helps us to assess how well we are doing overall.

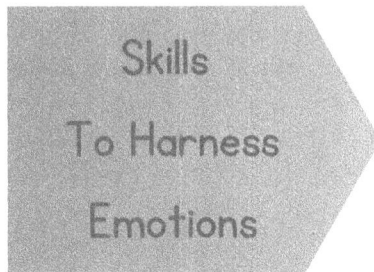

Skills
To Harness
Emotions

DOI: 10.4324/9781003581994-4

Theories of emotions

Our emotional lives are a potentially rich source of happiness and well-being.

> *Evolutionary psychologists have studied our emotional lives, questioning:*
> *What is the purpose of our emotions?*
> *How do they help us to survive and thrive?*

Our emotions are essentially an unconscious process, yet they are powerful motivating forces that prepare us for action. Because they are spontaneous biological processes, we need to learn the skills to manage and control them. We socialise our children to do this throughout their childhood, dealing with the terrible twos being an extreme example; it is an essential part of raising our children.

The feelings we have are how we interpret the emotions we experience: in other words, we experience a biological emotion, then we have a thought about it, we interpret it. Once we have thought about our feelings, we can make decisions about what to do, we can take action. This sequence of biological emotion, interpretation of feeling, and move to action is the essential foundation of cognitive behavioural therapy, one of the most popular and effective human change technologies in use today, in a wide variety of ways and settings.

Our emotional lives are fundamental to our happiness and overall well-being, and how we teach and learn the skills to control our emotions is intensively studied and measured.

> *We should judge the state of the world by how far people are enjoying their lives, by the amount of happiness there is.*
> *Everybody's happiness matters equally.*
> *Lord Richard Layard in "Can we be happier?"[1]*

Our emotions are telling us something, and when we listen in we can use this understanding to take control, and be at our best when we need to be.

There are essentially two key theories of emotions that will be helpful for our purposes. The first, established in the 1970s, asserts that there are five basic emotions. Some of these are brought to life in the characters in the film *Inside Out!*

> *Joy Anger Grief Fear Happiness[2]*

Later research added disgust, to make six basic emotions that are universal, because they could be seen in facial expressions. Further research added surprise to this list, then later again pride, shame, embarrassment, and excitement.

The second theory identified combined emotions, blends of feelings, for example, joy and trust together create love. Other emotions were defined as amusement, contempt, contentment, embarrassment, excitement, guilt, pride, relief, and satisfaction.

One of the many problems of research into emotions is that the more there are, the harder it is to study them effectively.

Because there are so many words that describe the way we feel, we often find ourselves using the same small range, or we clump them together, for example: I felt so angry and upset. The difference between these two is significant particularly when noticing the behaviour associated with them. The more precise we can be about our feelings and their intensity, the better we can communicate that to others.

The study of emotions is challenging in many dimensions. Fortunately, some researchers have taken a more pragmatic view, and developed some usable frameworks that help us to think about how we can talk and work with our feelings.

We will focus on a few accessible and powerful ways to educate ourselves and our children on how to develop and manage our emotional well-being as the first foundational skill of psychological fitness.

The happiness pie[3]

Positive psychology helps us to understand the behaviours and the actions that we can take to improve our well-being, to feel good, and live well. Researchers developed a neat pie chart to help us think about the control we have over how well we are doing. It concluded that:

- 50% of our happiness is determined by our genetic makeup,
- 10% by our life circumstances, the big things we can't change very easily, where we were born for example.
- 40% by the intentional actions we take.

In one way this chart offers an empowering message: wow! forty percent of my personal happiness is down to me, through the decisions I make and the actions I take.

In another way it could be disabling: what if we don't act because we don't know what to do? If we don't have the know-how, we can feel bewildered and stuck. Does this mean that we don't have capacity or resilience?

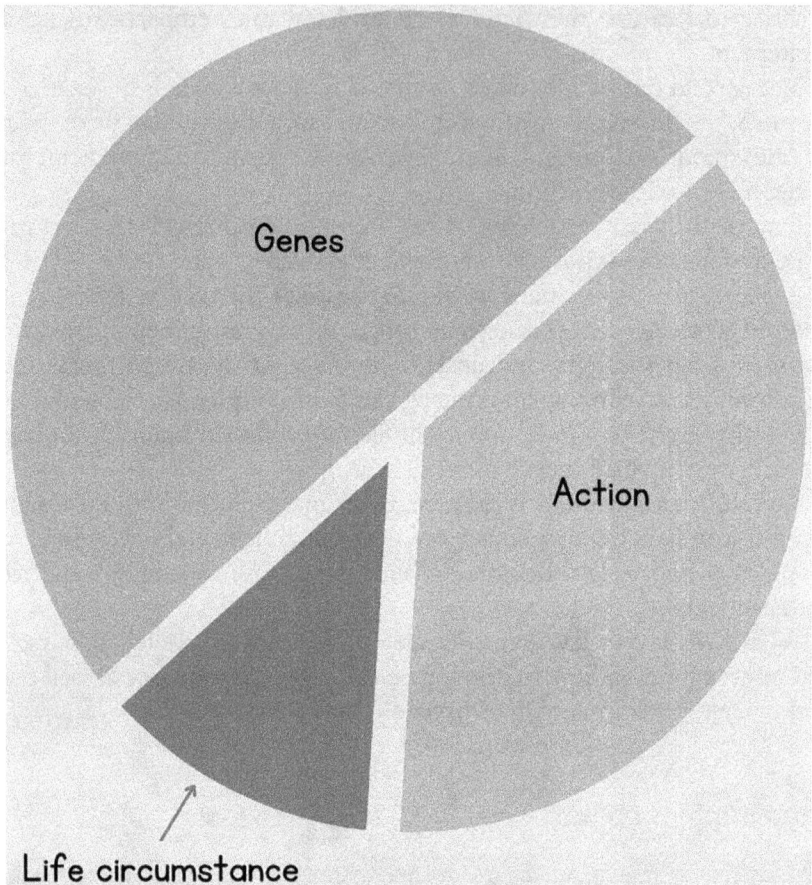

Genes

Action

Life circumstance

Of course it doesn't. It's all very well knowing that forty percent of our happiness is connected to the choices we make for ourselves and the actions we take, but that requires knowledge, skills, and know-how. We feel confident dealing with setbacks and challenges when we have skills that we trust, and, most importantly, we also feel equipped to flourish and thrive, to feel good and live well.

The role of positive emotions

Back when our hunter–gatherer ancestors were struggling to survive, responding instinctively to their negative emotions was life critical.

Thankfully we don't have quite the same level of threat, but we have held onto a bias to the negative. As we have evolved, and our understanding of the brain has developed, it was found that our positive emotions were just as important as our negative feelings. It is not just about the desire to feel good: most of us dream of relaxed and calm days away from the day job and the mundane routines. Positive emotion is more than that: when we experience it, we expand and broaden our capacities to create more possibilities.

Our ancestors didn't invent useful tools or decorate the cave walls with paintings when they were worrying about being eaten by tigers. They only had capacity for those creative activities when they felt safe and free from worry.

> *Positive emotions are not just something to pay attention to when all the important things have been ticked off.*

Research has shown that they lead to a host of intellectual, physical, social and psychological benefits.[4]

Intellectual capacity:

- We think more creatively
- We think more laterally
- We can solve problems better
- We learn faster

Physical capacity:

- We live longer
- We have better cardiovascular health
- We have better coordination

Social capacity:

- We have stronger, richer, relationships
- We can make new friends and keep them

Psychological capacity

- We are more resilient to setbacks
- We are more optimistic
- We are more likely to set goals and then reach them

Positive emotions make a big difference. It's not about feeling happy all the time but recognising when we can take deliberate, intentional steps to experience positive emotion. It's a coping strategy to ensure we can thrive.

Taking action: strategies for harnessing positive emotions

Positive emotions are just as important to notice as the negative, and noticing how we are feeling, leaning in to recognise, identify, and acknowledge them, is vital in understanding ourselves. Our feelings are a signal, telling us to do something: laugh, withdraw, defend, attack, plan. They are a powerful source of energy, creativity, and empathy. Rather than avoid or ignore our feelings, we can use them in deliberate and intentional ways that fall into five main categories:

1. **Bodily:** using our body to create calm energy, to relax and release positive emotion. Strategies include breathing, mindfulness, calm stillness, muscle relaxation.
2. **Cognitive**: using our thinking brain to distract us to reframe and channel our energy and create calmness. Strategies include mental games, distraction, journalling, and dedicated focus elsewhere.
3. **Connection:** using our social capacities to remind us we are not alone and that we are needed by others. Feeling close and valued is a fundamental human need and critical for our mental well-being. Strategies include talking to others, about problems, for sure, but also sharing our lived experiences, and seeking new perspectives on our lives.
4. **Imagination:** using the wonder of our brains to imagine anything we like, using all our senses to conjure stories and pictures that we can lose ourselves in, manage difficult emotions, set aside reality, relax and feel safe in. Strategies include visualisation, play, creative writing, mental and sensory safe spaces.
5. **Physical:** using the body to create physical movement to release natural chemicals such as serotonin and endorphins that boost mood and help concentration. Physical activity provides stress relief which is good for physical health such as coordination, and cardiovascular health and improved sleep. Strategies include everything from standing up regularly, walking, dancing, gardening, using weights, stretching, swimming.

Journal writing is an interesting way to harness our feelings, combining imagination and cognition. It's easy, effective, and straightforward. The benefits of journal writing are well founded and known to improve mind and body in a host of ways. Here are just a few examples that are of particular relevance here:

- Self-awareness
- Understanding others
- Understanding relationships
- Leaving problems behind
- Gaining perspective
- Boosting your mood
- Calming and clearing your mind
- Releasing pent-up feelings
- Releasing tension

The purpose of a journal is to record our feelings and thoughts about what's going on in our lives. Writing about the ups and downs, particularly if we don't understand what has happened and why, can have a calming and clarifying effect that devotees describe as miraculous. When we write down what is in our heads, we can see things more objectively. As it's for our eyes only, we can write in any way we wish, jotting words down without the need to worry about prose style or perfect punctuation. Journalling is such a simple process, with powerful results. All you need is a pen and paper, which works better than typing on a computer, for mysterious reasons.

Life can be tough, and the changeable external environment we face as we go about our everyday lives means we need more than one way to harness and manage our positive emotions. We need different strategies that work in different situations because the idea is not to save up these ideas for the weekend or holidays but to build them into our everyday lives. What we do at home won't always be useful at work. Something we have time for during the weekend becomes redundant during the busy week. We need to think about finding a range of things that would fit into each category or different length of time, one minute, five minutes, ten minutes. Things that we can do on the spot, **and** in a more planned way – things that work for us over the course of a day or a week, as needed.

The energy and emotions grid[5]

The following grid shows the intersection between energy, which can be high or low, and emotions, which can be positive or negative. That creates four quadrants, four different combinations of energy and emotions.

Once you've absorbed that, look at the list of emotions and categorise them. For example, consider the first word, optimistic. Decide whether feeling optimistic is high energy or low energy and whether it is positive or negative and then position it on the grid in the relevant quadrant. Then repeat for all the emotions.

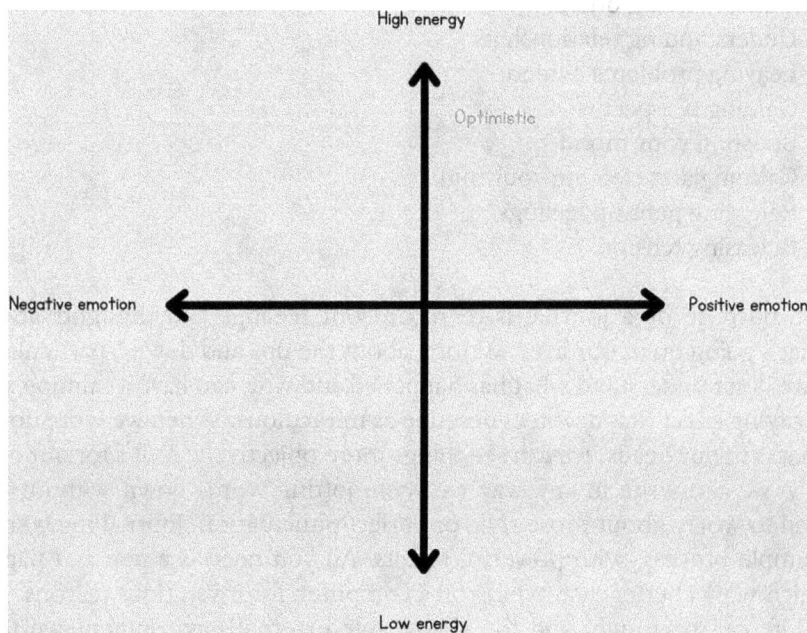

High energy

Optimistic

Negative emotion ← → Positive emotion

Low energy

Optimistic	Defiant	Exhausted	Carefree	Miserable	
Defensive	Excited	Enthusiastic	Rejected		
Irritable	Annoyed	Sad	Calm	Confident	
Fearful	Bored	Engaged	Happy	Worried	
Relaxed	Proud	Depressed	Angry	Thankful	Anxious
Empty	Peaceful	Frustrated	Receptive	Incensed	
Hopeless	Stimulated	Impatient	Serene	At ease	Envious
Tired	Mellow	Astonished	Relieved	Lonely	

★★★

Now compare your completed grid with the one in Figure 3.4. Notice any differences to where you have placed them. If some are different, focus on thinking about how it feels to experience that emotion. Is it high or low energy? Is it on the positive or negative side?

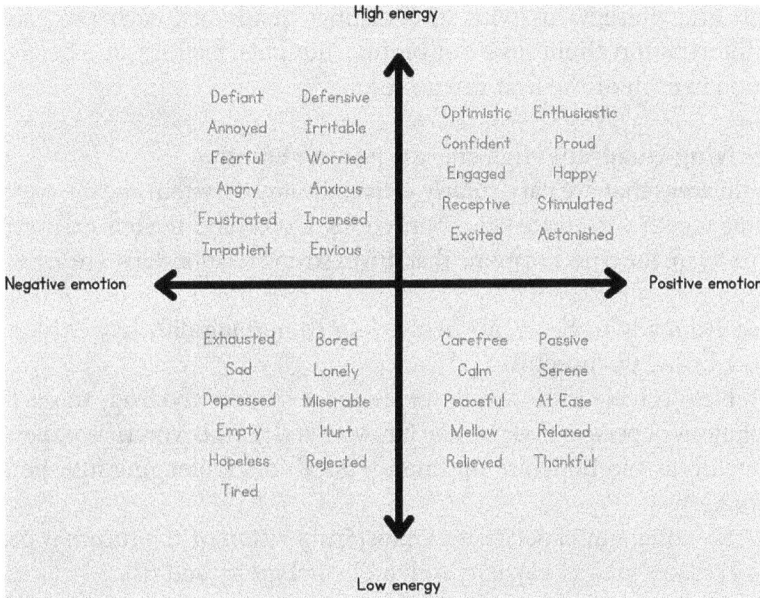

Figure 3.4

This intersection between emotions, energy, and performance was originally developed decades ago by sports psychologists to help athletes prepare for peak performance in competition. It has since been applied beyond the sports field, at work, at home, as a leader, worker, mother, brother, teenager studying for exams, indeed anyone.

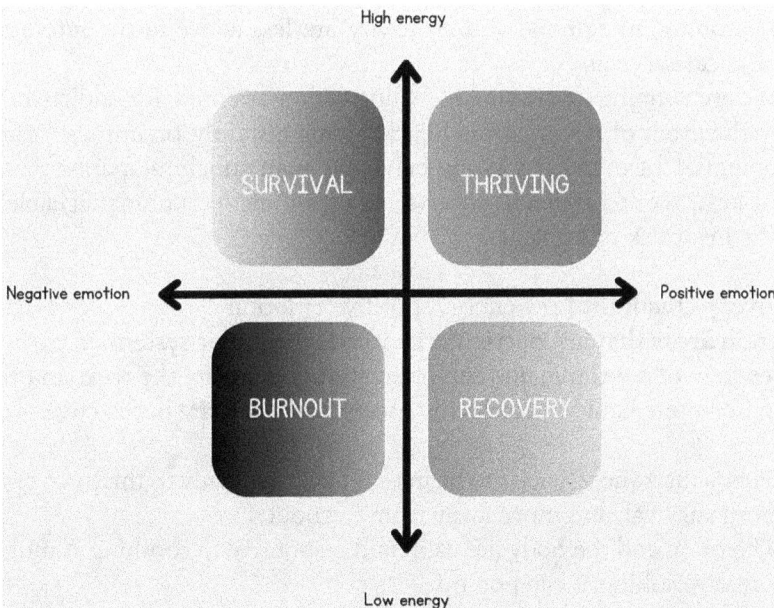

The grid presents us with four distinct quadrants, each providing us with information about how our brains, thoughts, feelings, and behaviours function in each of the four categories.

Thriving Quadrant High energy / positive emotion

Brain areas that are particularly active: the limbic system and the cortex are working together to create new connections. Dopamine, the reward hormone, and oxytocin, the trust hormone that drives strong relationships, are active.

- We are ready to be at our best, to do something difficult, challenging, new, brave, purposeful.
- Problem-solving is enhanced; we are more creative and likely to see lateral solutions or perspectives; we can innovate and think beyond past experience.
- Our mind and body are optimised, good for challenging interpersonal situations.
- In this zone, our capacity for an inspiring vision of the future is present and creates greater capacity to handle ambiguity and risk.

Survival Quadrant High energy / negative emotion

Brain areas that are particularly active: the limbic system, particularly the amygdala, and the brain stem – adrenalin, the survival hormone, is flooding our bodies.

- We are feeling under threat, vague or actual, and our bodies are preparing for fight, flight, freeze, faint, fawn. We are ready for anything.
- Reasoning, imagining, and creativity are less active in the interests of physical survival.
- We are running on adrenalin, feeling action oriented. It's addictive.
- In the event of an amygdala hijack, acting instantly, on impulse, there is potential for overreaction and behaving in an unhelpful manner.
- At best, we are driven to survive. At worst, life feels unmanageable and we are at risk of burnout.

Recovery Quadrant Low energy / positive emotion

Brain areas that are particularly active: the limbic system, in particular the centers of soothing, and the brain stem. Oxytocin, the trust and relaxation hormone, and serotonin, the happy hormone, are both active.

- This is the zone we need to be in to recover, be ready to thrive, to restore from survival, and move away from burnout.
- The brain and the body are calm and responsive to soothing stimuli.
- Creative solutions can pop up.

- We are more open to those around us.
- Recovery can be brief interludes in our day and longer activities we plan for the evening, weekend, or holiday.
- Good-quality rest and sleep are a fundamental form of recovery.

Burnout Quadrant Low energy / negative emotion

Brain areas that are particularly active: in the limbic system and the cortex, neural pathways have become stuck. The brain and the body are exhausted and run down. High cortisol, the stress hormone, has flooded the system.

- Stress or strain over time can take you to the burnout zone, impacting your performance and your health.
- The brain is limited as negative thinking habits prevail.
- It's more difficult to solve problems in this zone than any other as creativity and energy are missing.
- Experiencing negative, low-energy feelings is a reminder that we haven't been prioritising recovery, and recovery is our way out of burnout.

Understanding the four quadrants can be useful in helping to take control and decide what to prioritise. If we can find the right balance, we can use recovery to thrive when needed, particularly during the hard driving survival moments.

There is not a perfect blend of how much time to prioritise or where to be on the framework because that will depend on all sorts of things, including what is happening around us. For example, during a difficult time, a family illness, a redundancy or change at work, moving house, these will all have an impact. The way to take more control of the external factors is to find enough balance in recovery.

These are not descriptions of good or bad states to feel; all can be both helpful and unhelpful depending on the situation. For example:

- Feeling frustrated might be useful when we want to extend our capacity: to learn something new, to become better, stronger, fitter. People under pressure, for example, might be in survival mode when they are competing against high performers, or when they have moved up a level.
- Feeling confident, engaged, happy is helpful when we need to perform at our peak, to be in the best possible place.
- Feeling calm, at peace, is helpful for essential recovery, to allow our bodies and minds to rest and prepare for new challenges.
- Feeling sad is not something we might think of as useful, but if we have experienced loss, bereavement for example, then expressing our sadness is necessary.

Something for you to try

Think about what percentage of time you have spent in each of the quadrants of the grid in the last week. Take your time to reflect on this and be honest with yourself. Don't dwell on the reasons why; the activity here is to develop a general sense of how your life circumstances and the decisions you make determine where you spend time.

1. In the first graph, think back over the last few weeks and write in the approximate percentage of time that you have been spending in each of the four quadrants.

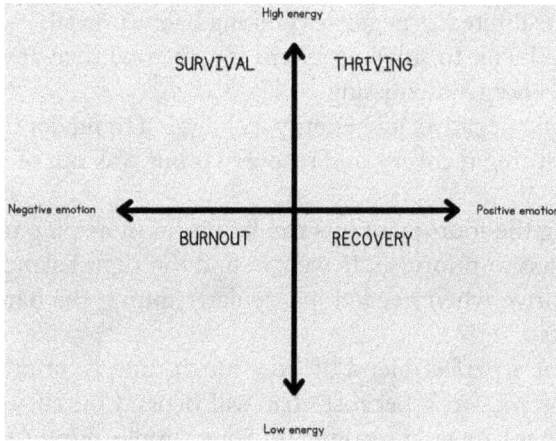

2. In the second graph write in the amount of time that, if you had a magic wand, would be the right amount **of time for you right now.**

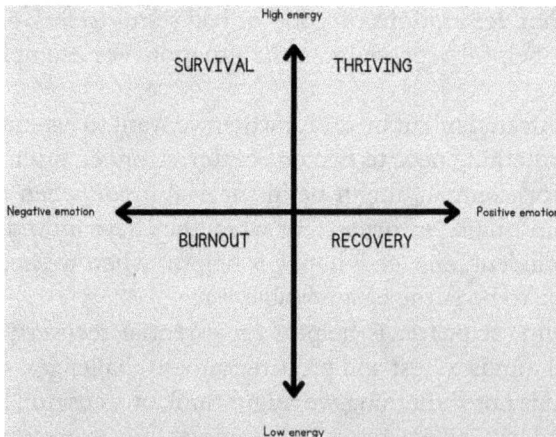

Next think about the sorts of activities that you do that allow you to experience recovery emotions: feeling carefree, calm, relaxed, at ease, mellow. Be as specific as possible. Consider what it is about the activity that means you feel at ease; what is it that creates peace for you?

Finally think about how you can take more control of where you are on the grid. Use the strategies to consider if there are things that you do, or used to do, or only do at particular times. What *could* you do, what might you enjoy learning more about, what has interested you in the past? Again, be as specific as possible.

The aim is to have a range of recovery strategies, things that can work across different aspects of your everyday life, and for different time lengths. For example, things that take just thirty seconds, or two minutes, or five minutes as well as longer periods of recovery, like an afternoon in nature, or a day off.

Practising the strategies

If the strategies are new to you, tweak them until they become a familiar part of your tool kit. Think about the action you can take to spend time in recovery when you need to recharge for a few minutes before the next moment when you need to be thriving, and to help you out of burnout in the times when life presents the difficult moments.

Use the activity to model to teenagers that you value recovery. Name the action you take and let them see you are taking those peaceful, still moments. Find recovery moments together and then talk about how they help.

> *Recovery is vital for performing at our best in the moments that we need to.*

It is not something to aim for all the time, as being at our best is not necessary all the time, and it is impossible anyway. Avoid setting the bar too high, for too much of the time. Recovery helps to recognise the role that positive emotions take in our lives. It gives us the permission and motivation to take action to feel calm and relaxed. We should not wait for those moments to come our way; we could plan, pursue, and prioritise the time to recover, and create self-awareness about the things that make us feel at ease, serene, and peaceful. Then we can build actions into every day. These are not wasted time, or being lazy, or not important; people who are mentally resilient and emotionally strong value and prioritise recovery.

To illustrate how the skills and strategies in this book can be used as part of everyday life, we will be reading about the experiences of an imaginary family: Carla and Pete and their children, Lily, aged eight, Ella, twelve, and Joe, fourteen.

Carla is forty and works full time and looks after most of the household duties. She has a nursing degree and now holds a demanding corporate role at a private health insurer. Carla shoulders the responsibility for the family, making decisions about holidays, social events, kids clubs, schools. Looking after her family's health is important to her. She eats well and goes to the gym. Occasionally she has nights out with her friends, and sometimes a weekend away. Carla would love to have hobbies, but she doesn't have time. She dreams of reading more, maybe learning a language, or painting; she has a talent for art.

Pete is forty-three and manager for a large warehouse company. He has staff responsibility and management targets, so it's a demanding job, often with long hours. He happily leaves the social calendar to Carla, but does meet his friends from time to time. He coaches his son's football team, which takes up a chunk of his spare time. He is good at DIY around the house and helps Carla with family and domestic tasks when he can.

Imagine this

It had been a busy week at work for Carla, and at home, as Pete was away at a work conference. Thankfully, he'd be back tomorrow. Carla had been managing the usual load: the after-school activities, and juggling the complicated schedules of pickup and drop-offs. She was feeling overwhelmed. She'd hardly slept last night, worrying about a rumour she'd heard at work about possible redundancies.

She picked up Lily from her after-school club and was relieved to get home. She sent her daughter upstairs to change out of her school uniform. Needing a cup of tea and a moment to herself, she headed for the kitchen, and her heart sank as she saw the breakfast dishes still on the table. She'd been in such a rush this morning, getting everyone ready and in the car, she hadn't had time to clear up. As she tidied up, she felt annoyed and sorry for herself. Household chores were endless: looking after the children, managing a full-time job, and on her own most of the time as well, it was all too much for her. She felt tears rising and swallowed hard. Ella and Joe would be home soon, and the place would be chaos. So much for having a moment to herself.

As she went into the hall, she skidded on one of Lily's ballet shoes, falling with a hard bump, just as her daughter arrived at the bottom of the stairs. This sent her over the edge.

Furiously she shouted. "Lily! I told you before to put your shoes away! Don't you ever think about anyone but yourself? Why can't you do as you're told? Do you think I don't have enough to do? It's time you grew up young lady and cleared up after yourself. You're not a baby." Lily started crying. Carla felt dreadful, taking out her anger and fatigue on her little girl like that. She said sorry, and hugged her tight. When Joe and Ella arrived a little later, she felt so tired that she gave them all a snack and, unusually, left them watching TV.

Then she went up to her bedroom, and lay on the bed, feeling terrible about herself and furious with the world. I can't keep doing it all, she said to herself. Tears came to her eyes, as she thought of her mum, who had died shortly after Joe was born. "I want my Mum," she whispered and cried. As her tears flowed, she felt relieved to let go of some of her emotions and that helped her feel better. In the bathroom, she washed her face, looked at herself in the mirror, and said to her reflection: "You're burned out, time to do something to recover."

Carla thought she had a decent self-care regime, her me time. She went regularly to the gym, the hairdressers, and the beauty salon, and she enjoyed the occasional night out with a girlfriend. But as she thought about it now, she realised that finding the time for those things could also be a pressure, tasks to fit in, a to-do list, rather than space and time for recovery. If only there was some way of resetting her energy and mood that didn't take up so much time, something more immediate.

Taking a deep breath in, she was reminded of mindfulness and meditation. Way back, before the kids, yoga and mindfulness were hobbies of hers. So was journal writing which she loved, another thing that she had no time for now. All those great ways of resetting her body and mind, how could she have forgotten?

Remembering the techniques, she sat comfortably, feeling present, noticing where her body connected to the floor, and closed her eyes. She took a slow deep breath in and held it. Then she slowly released her breath until she reached that moment where she was neither breathing in nor out. Then she repeated, a slow deep breath in, hold one, two, three, four . . . and slowly release. And again. Once more.

The intentional breathing settled her. It was that quick, just a few minutes and her body felt relaxed, her energy more balanced, and her mind clearer. She felt good, so she sat for a few minutes longer, reflecting on how this simple, quick breathing pattern could change things so fast.

Heading downstairs, she went to join her children. Lily climbed on her lap and Carla hugged her. "Sorry for shouting at you earlier, mummy had a stressful day, but I'm feeling a lot better now." Lily snuggled in.

Ella said, "I saw you upstairs, because I peeked my head in, and you were meditating! Is that what helped you feel better?"

"Yes," Carla said. "It's something I used to do when I was younger, but I had forgotten how good it felt. Have you ever done anything like that?"

"We tried breathing exercises at school. Sometimes we do them before the start of a lesson, especially after lunch to help the boys calm down," Ella said.

"Maybe it's something we could do together in future?" Carla suggested.

"Maybe, yeah," Lily said.

"Joe, what about you. Fancy it?" Carla said, but he was too engrossed in his screen to answer.

That was one for another day, she thought.

Summary

Recovery is essential for being at our best, to thrive in the moments we need to. It's also vital for restoring and recuperating before, during, and after difficult situations. We have learnt that:

- Thinking about the things we do to spend time in recovery is time well spent.
- Don't wait until burnout to think about recovery because our brain is not able to be creative.
- Short one-, two-, five-minute actions can be the difference between you thriving or surviving a situation.

Activities for teenagers

As we've already said, remember to be thoughtful about when to introduce these activities. You know your teenager best, so you decide what, when, and how to share the ideas. Make it an authentic learning moment, the same way you might teach them about anything.

Emotions

You could use this activity when your children are bored, or when you want them to take a break from something, including electronic devices. It is important that we can feel comfortable talking about our feelings, and that starts with learning the words that describe emotions. Then we can build awareness about how they can be experienced and the sorts of situations when experiencing emotions is "normal" or expected: for example, it's normal to feel happy when we are given a gift, or sad when we argue with a friend, or guilty if we have said something in a clumsy way and caused harm. Knowing what is "normal" or what we are expected to feel also helps us to recognise when we are experiencing emotions that are unusual or not normal to us, which acts as a signal to seek help.

> **This is intended as a fun activity to explore our emotions:**

Without using anything other than your own mind think of as many words as possible that describe emotions.

Invite other children and family members to join in and see who can think of the most.

Now use the list of emotions to:

- Think of a song that makes you feel happy and, if possible, play it.
- Write down five things that help you feel low-energy, positive emotions.
- Pick ten emotions from the list. Five high energy and five low energy.
  - Draw ten circles and add faces that represent the emotion (e.g. surprised might have big wide eyes and mouth open).
  - Next to the completed face write what else might be happening in the body when feeling this emotion (e.g. embarrassed: the skin feels warm, going red in the face).
  - Then think about the small everyday reasons that someone might feel this emotion.

Emotion	Complete the faces by drawing how the emotion would look	What might be happening in the body when feeling this emotion? For example, embarrassed: the skin feels hot, the face is red.	Think of one small everyday reason that someone might feel this emotion.
Excited			
Worried			
Carefree			

The purpose of the following activities is to introduce different ways to experience the low energy and positive emotions of the recovery zone: how to feel calm, be still, focused, and at ease, to recharge and recover.

3–7 breathing

Sit on a chair with both feet flat on the floor; get comfortable but avoid slouching.

Closing your eyes is best, or find a point on the floor directly in front of you to focus on.

Breathe in 1, 2, 3 and out 1, 2, 3. Repeat two or three times.

Now slow the breathing down further, this time to a count of four.

Breathe in 1, 2, 3, 4 and out 1, 2, 3, 4. After a couple of times go even slower and count to 5.

Breathe in 1, 2, 3, 4, 5 and out 1, 2, 3, 4, 5. Repeat.

Then count to six. Breathe in 1, 2, 3, 4, 5, 6 and out 1, 2, 3, 4, 5, 6.

And, finally to a count of seven. Breathe in 1, 2, 3, 4, 5, 6, 7 and out 1, 2, 3, 4, 5, 6, 7.

Water soother

Water has natural properties that can have a soothing effect on both mind and body.

Running a warm bubble bath and then cooling off afterwards in the shower can make you feel refreshed and stimulate your body flow.

Alternating between warmer and colder water in the shower can achieve the same benefits.

Holding ice cubes in your hands until they melt could also be a good way to calm down and focus on something else.

Mental games

Countdown from one hundred in threes – 100, 97, 94, 91, 88, 85 . . . keep going until you get to 0.

List all the members of your favourite sports team.

Think of an animal for every letter in the alphabet: A for antelope, B for bear, C for cat . . .

Visualise dealing with strong emotions

Imagine stepping outside of your mind. Imagine climbing some of the stairs to a balcony above and looking down on your situation below, so you can see the situation from a distance. Without trying to change anything, just seeing it from above, you are far away from it, not directly involved. Think about the advice that you would give to deal with this situation in the best way.

Visualise kindness

Sit upright, get comfortable, and feel present in your seat. Place your feet flat on the ground. Take three slow deep breaths, and as you do, notice your feet connected to the ground where you sit.

Think of someone who makes you happy, a person or a pet. Bring them, and how you feel about them, clearly into your mind and choose a colour to represent them. Take three deep breaths in and out.

Now imagine sending the lovely colour to a friend, or someone who needs kindness, and then see this person smiling, when they receive the colour. As you do, take three deep breaths in and out.

Next imagine sending the colour to someone you don't know so well, and see them smiling when they receive it. As you do, take three deep breaths in and out.

Now imagine sharing your lovely colour with everyone around you and let's fill this room with your colour. Smile and take three long deep breaths in and out.

Finger breathing

Sit upright in your chair, get comfortable, but feel present in your seat.

With your forefinger, trace around your thumb starting from your wrist, as you get to the top of your thumb, pause, before tracing down the other side.

Continue tracing each finger, pausing at the top before tracing down the side, all the way across your hand.

Now repeat that again but this time add some breathing. As you trace up to the top of your thumb breathe in slowly through your nose and out slowly through your mouth.

Continue tracing each finger, pausing at the top to breathe in slowly through your nose and out slowly through your mouth as you trace down each side. Continue finger breathing all the way across your hand.

Hand clapping

Clap your hands in time as you count slowly down from ten; each second number, the clap must get quieter and by zero the clap produces no noise.

When you reach zero, put all your attention into your hands.

- Notice what is going on there.
- What sensations do you feel?
- What's the temperature like?

As your hands go back to feeling normal, give them a little shake and blow gently across them.

Managing your sleep

The circadian rhythm is a twenty-four-hour cycle, from sunrise to sunset. It's our body clock: some people are more awake at night and sleep in, while others go to bed early and rise early. These two types are sometimes called larks or owls.

There are two types of sleep:

REM (rapid eye movement), when the body switches off and the brain receives extra blood, and processes information. For our teenagers, this is a busy time:

- Growth hormones are released
- Memories are consolidated and stored

- Brain cells are repaired and cleaned up
- Social and emotional abilities are stored

As we age, we spend less time in REM sleep. Keeping a sleep diary for a couple of weeks is helpful. Think about:

- What time you naturally wake up or are woken up by an alarm.
- What do you usually do first when you wake up?
- What is your routine when you're first out of bed?

Non-REM sleep is made up of three stages. This is the restful and restorative sleep where your body is being repaired. Non-REM sleep lowers muscle tone, body temperature, heart rate, and blood pressure.

- Stage N1 is light sleep; you're nodding off but can be easily woken by a slight sound or movement.
- Stage N2 is a deeper sleep; you're still aware of your surroundings, but if you're not disturbed, it would lead to deep sleep.
- Stage N3 is deep sleep, when you're hard to wake up.

Think about what happens during the day. Note down anything that would impact your sleep, such as:

- Taking short naps
- The amount of physical activity you do and when
- Your eating pattern

Then note down your evening routine:

- What time do you usually start winding down?
- What specifically do you do and at what time?

Top tips for making healthy changes to your sleep routine:

- Take a relaxing bath or shower
- Turn off digital devices
- Create a relaxing bedroom environment: lower the lights, listen to mood music or white noise
- Read something that relaxes you
- Have a hot drink, but avoid caffeine and sweet drinks
- Build some calm and focussed exercises into the routine: use 4–7–8 breathing, or something similar

The 4–7–8 breathing exercise

Practise this breathing technique during the day, at different times. To begin with it might feel a little strange, even make you feel lightheaded, but that will pass.

As it becomes more familiar, it will feel more useful, and something you can do to help you sleep, or calm down and relax.

Find a comfortable place to sit, then:

1. Put your tongue against the back of your top teeth and keep it there.
2. Inhale . . . then exhale fully through your mouth, not moving your tongue, making a "whoosh" sound, and purse your lips, as if you are going to whistle as you exhale fully. This is a big breath out.
3. Close your lips, inhale through your nose for a count of four, 1, 2, 3, 4.
4. Now hold your breath for a count of eight, 1, 2, 3, 4, 5, 6, 7, 8.
5. Exhale fully through your mouth, making a "whoosh" sound for a count of eight, 1, 2, 3, 4, 5, 6, 7, 8.

Repeat steps 1–5 again, three more times.

Notes

1 Layard R. (2020). *Can We Be Happier? Evidence and Ethics*. A Pelican Book.
2 Cherry K. (2010). *The Everything Psychology Book: Explore the Human Psyche and Understand Why We Do the Things We Do*. Everything Series, 2nd ed.
3 Sheldon KM, Lyubomirsky S. (2019). Revisiting the Sustainable Happiness Model and Pie Chart: Can Happiness Be Successfully Pursued? *The Journal of Positive Psychology*. https://doi.org/10.1080/17439760.2019.1689421
4 Fredrickson BL. (2004, September 29). The Broaden-and-Build Theory of Positive Emotions. *Philosophical Transactions of the Royal Society B: Biological Sciences*, 359(1449), 1367–1378. https://doi.org/10.1098/rstb.2004.1512. PMID: 15347528; PMCID: PMC1693418.
5 Loehr J, Schwartz T. (2006). *The Power of Full Engagement: Managing Energy, Not Time, Is the Key to High Performance and Personal Renewal*. Gabler. https://doi.org/10.1007/978-3-8349-9251-2_17

Slow and steady   **4**

The link between thoughts, feelings, and behaviour

Our understanding of what it means to be psychologically resilient has changed considerably over the last seventy years, when it was seen as the ability to return to normal after trauma.[1] It was believed that a person could not be resilient unless they had faced and overcome a significant setback, adverse situation, or traumatic event.

Several decades later this definition broadened to include the capacity to cope with all types of even quite minor difficulties, with the emphasis still on the notion of recovery.

The focus then changed radically, switching from a medical idea that post-traumatic stress disorder could be resolved or healed, to an educational focus on how developing the skills to overcome even quite minor challenges could lead to enhanced mental resilience: post-traumatic *growth*.

Positive psychology[2] identified capabilities that could be taught, mastered, and measured. The skills needed to bounce forward from conflict or failure are the very same skills as those needed to realise our potential to thrive, to seek opportunity, and to be the best version of ourselves.

ABC Skill

DOI: 10.4324/9781003581994-5

One of the most powerful ways of managing our emotions is understanding the link between our thoughts, feelings, and behaviours.

This concept is the engine room of mental resilience. As we tune into what we believe is true about what happens to us, we can slow things down and take a steady look at what is really going on. Then we can decide what to do next.

When we can deal with difficulty we are developing and growing our capacity. Self-awareness is the basis for solving many of the problems we face. If we don't understand ourselves, it will be difficult to decide what to do for the best. How can we explain what matters most to us, and how can others help and support us? Mental resilience is not a one-size-fits-all concept because at the heart is a unique individual, living life through a personal lens, so how we all work through that will vary. Self-awareness develops as we look inward to understand ourselves better. This is one of the most valuable and useful things we can do, when it comes to being psychologically fit.

Something to try

Complete the table and then reflect on the following questions:

Reflecting on Resilience		
	When I am resilient	When I am not resilient
How I look to others …		
I feel …		
My response is …		
I believe the situation to be …		

- What do you notice?
- Reflect on the things that impact your resilience.
- Do you recognise patterns or particular situations, people, or triggers that impact your capacity to be resilient?

The ABC of mental resilience

We tend to think that events lead us to react the way we do: for example, I was stuck in a traffic jam, and it ruined my day. But it wasn't the jam that ruined my day, and was my day really ruined?

Things happen. We are held up in traffic and some of us might start to feel angry and beep our horns. Others might feel relaxed and turn on their radio or listen to their favourite podcast. Someone else might feel anxious and sit clasping their forehead.

That's three different responses to the same situation.

We used to understand this as a simple stimulus and response dynamic: something happens and there is a consequence. We feel something and we react.

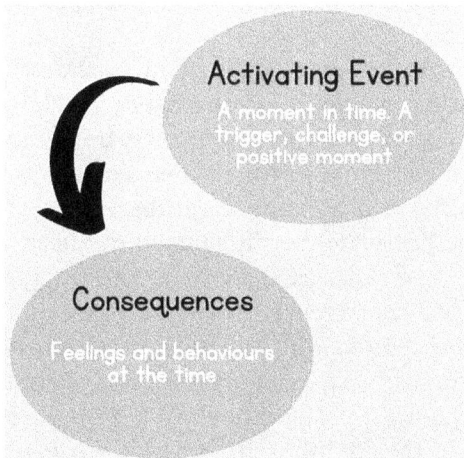

However, this can't be completely true because different people in exactly the same situation react differently. So, why is that?

The reason is that we create a story, a set of thoughts about the activating event, and it's the beliefs we have in that moment that leads to how we feel and behave.

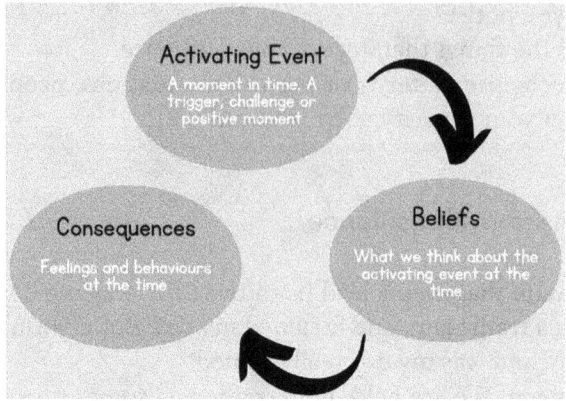

This is the ABC of mental resilience, the foundational skill that helps us understand that there is a link between our beliefs, and how we feel and behave. This allows us to slow the situation down to understand our response.

The ABC skill is designed to sharpen the clarity of:

- What actually happened?
- What did I believe about what happened?
- What did I feel and how did I react to what happened?

Let's examine the components of the ABC in more detail.

A is the **activating event**. Something happens. This is the who, what, where, and when of the matter. It's a moment in time, and if we were to take a photograph, we could agree on what happened, who was there, and when and where it was. This is an account of the observable facts of the situation.

B is the **beliefs**. These are the thoughts in our head at the moment of the activating event. It's what we think right then and there, like a personal internal radio station that's telling us what's going on. The thoughts are either explaining the reasons why something has happened, or what might happen next. The beliefs we have in the moment lead to our consequences.

C is the **consequences**. It's both how we feel on the inside and how we react on the outside, the emotions that we experience in that moment, and the observable external behaviour. This is what other people see us doing, for example, beeping our horn, turning on our radio, clasping our forehead.

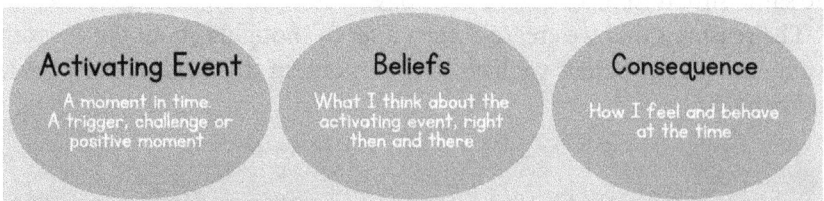

The ABC skill is super simple to learn. However, using it can be a little harder.

As we are more attuned to noticing the A and C rather than what we think, this foundational skill takes practice. Mostly the ABC is helpful to use when we are uncomfortable with how we are feeling or behaving, and it can help us take some control by recognising that our beliefs are driving how we react. It is also worth noting that it can also be useful when we have consequences that are working for us. For example our teenager responds favourably to a request and tuning into the detail helps us to understand the good moments so we can repeat it in future.

Something to try

The best way to learn this skill is to give it a go. Think of three to five situations, everyday occurrences, that might raise your temperature or leave you feeling a bit frustrated. Don't choose the long-standing family feud at this stage!

Read and reflect on the worksheet in Figure 4.6 to note down your examples.

> Think of some specific small everyday situations.
> Times when you were not happy with the way you handled it, or the way you felt, or you didn't get the outcome you expected.
> Use situations from different parts of your life, friends, family, at work, in the community.

1.

2.

3.

4.

5.

Figure 4.6

These worksheets help you practise the process of the ABC skill to slow things down. Later we will explore how you can take more control by reframing your beliefs, but at this stage, let's focus on learning the ABC.

Pick at least two of your examples to apply to the ABC slowing process. Use the worksheets to map out the situations.

Activating Event Who, What, Where, When	Beliefs What you thought at the time about the activating event	Consequences The emotion you felt and how you behaved at the time

Activating Event Who, What, Where, When	Beliefs What you thought at the time about the activating event	Consequences The emotion you felt and how you behaved at the time

Activating Event Who, What, Where, When	Beliefs What you thought at the time about the activating event	Consequences The emotion you felt and how you behaved at the time

Imagine this

It was 7 pm and Carla was trying to manage the evening activities. There was always so much to fit in: homework, dinner, bathtime, bedtime, preparing for tomorrow. Pete was late home, so she was alone. The kids had eaten earlier, but Carla still needed to cook dinner for her and Pete later. With any luck they could sit and have a quiet meal together and catch up.

She looked around the kitchen. It was a wreck, dishes everywhere, and school bags on the floor. Her kids never seemed to pick up after themselves. As if she didn't have enough to do.

"Hey Mum," Ella said. "Did you buy my cooking ingredients for tomorrow?" She opened the fridge and peered inside.

Carla frowned. "You should find everything you want in the larder."

"I can't see any eggs," Ella said.

Carla felt irritation rising through her. "You need to buck your ideas up Ella and stop being so idle."

"Mum! I'll be in trouble at school if I don't have all the ingredients."

Carla snapped. "Good, you should be in trouble. You're old enough to take some responsibility for making sure the ingredients are here, instead of leaving it till the last minute and expecting me to drop everything to run around after you."

"You said you'd buy them," Ella said and rushed out.

Carla was furious. We mollycoddle her, she thought. She takes me for granted. She should be doing more for herself at her age. Then she berated herself: I'm hopeless. I forgot the eggs. I can't remember everything. Pete should help me more. She sat at the kitchen table and put her head in her hands, depressed. She didn't move for half an hour.

Let's look at Carla's ABC:

Carla's ABC		
Activating Event Who, What, Where, When	Beliefs What Carla thought at the time about the activating event	Consequences The emotion Carla felt and how she behaved at the time
Carla is in the middle of a busy evening, on her own. She had fed the children but still had her and Pete's dinner to sort. There were dirty dishes in the kitchen, school bags on the floor. Ella came in and asked where the eggs were she needed for cooking class tomorrow. There were no eggs, and Ella said she would be in trouble at school and leaves the kitchen.	• We mollycoddle her. • She takes me for granted. • She should do more for herself at her age. • I'm hopeless. • Pete should help more.	Carla feels depressed and helpless. She sits down, puts her head in her hands, and doesn't move from that position for thirty minutes.

ABC watch-outs

There are a few things to watch out for with the ABC skill to make sure we use it correctly.

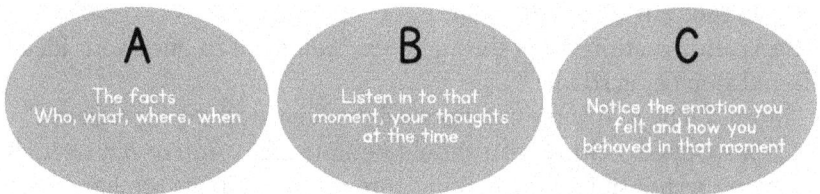

The first watch-out is to check that the A doesn't include any beliefs; we must only include what actually happened. If a photograph was taken of that moment, the facts could all be seen. Anything else will be beliefs, for example: a person is angry. It's difficult to know for sure that somebody is feeling angry unless they tell us. We may see behaviours that seem like anger, such as clutching their face or raising their voice. Although these are observable facts, the thought that the person is angry is our belief.

The activating event should only include the who, what, where, and when:

- WHO was there? The people involved.
- WHAT actually happened?
- WHERE did it take place?
- WHEN did it happen?

The second watch-out is when beliefs are presented as questions.

When we do this, it means we are not tuning in closely enough to what we were thinking at that moment. Beliefs are usually statements. For example: is my child in trouble? is a question. As a statement, that would be: my child is in trouble. That's more immediate, as you are tuning into what you were thinking right then and there.

Look back at your ABC worksheet and see if you have written a belief as a question. Listen closely to what you were really thinking. Ask yourself: what's the statement that sits below the question?

There is no need to share your ABC examples with anybody else. This is just self-reflection. It's part of developing self-awareness, to understand what we tend to think about in difficult situations. Over time we will start to notice patterns: sometimes I tend to think like this, and that makes me feel or behave in a certain way.

The third watch-out is to think about the C, the consequences. This should reveal both how we *feel*, and how we *behave*. We need at least one word that describes the emotion we are having right then and there. Our behaviour is external; it's what other people see us doing. This is part of building emotional awareness, as we learn to understand what we look like to others when we feel angry, or frustrated, or guilty, or happy, or excited.

Being aware of these watch-outs will allow you to use the ABC effectively, and to reflect on the purpose of the skill, which is to slow situations down. This is especially useful when we don't like how we are feeling or behaving, or when our consequences are not the outcomes we want. It is important to recognise that our beliefs may be in our head for a good reason, though sometimes our thoughts are unpleasant. We know we shouldn't think that, we know it's unkind, or not what we're supposed to think. We need to be honest with ourselves about what we are truly thinking in that moment when using the ABC.

Paying attention to our beliefs

When we tune into our thoughts, what we think in the moment, we can notice two types of beliefs:

- **Why beliefs**: thoughts about the reason why something has happened. I am stuck in a traffic jam because there are too many road works, or someone has been driving badly, or there has been an accident.
- **What next beliefs**: thoughts about the implications of what might happen. I am stuck in a traffic jam, and I am going to be late, I will let people down, I will be in trouble.

It is helpful to recognise this distinction to help us decide which of the skills might work best. For example, for why beliefs, *reframing* and *moving on* are the most helpful.

For what next beliefs, the strategies for *harnessing emotions* and *WoBbLe* would be the best. This is an important difference as we will see later.

The ABC is the cognitive behavioural link that expands the capacity to deal effectively with the adversities we face, both big and small. It shines a light on the place where we have some control. We can't always prevent situations happening to us, being stuck in a traffic jam, or forgetting the eggs because we have a million other things to think about. But understanding that the way we have interpreted the situation can be changed offers us an opportunity to take control.

Our beliefs matter in the moment, and they matter because situations do not happen in isolation. One moment leads to the next. Starting the day with a negative and unrealistic perspective might mean we carry that into the next moment and then throughout the day.

Imagine this

Carla got out of bed, tripped, and banged her toe because Pete had left his shoes somewhere she wasn't expecting them. She thought, I have to clean up after everybody. She felt agitated, missed the hairbrush on the floor, stepped on it, and screeched as a spike penetrated her foot. She hobbled to the bathroom to find an almost empty tube of toothpaste that took her longer than usual to squeeze out. She thought: nobody cares about my morning. She looked in the mirror and said out loud: "My day is doomed."

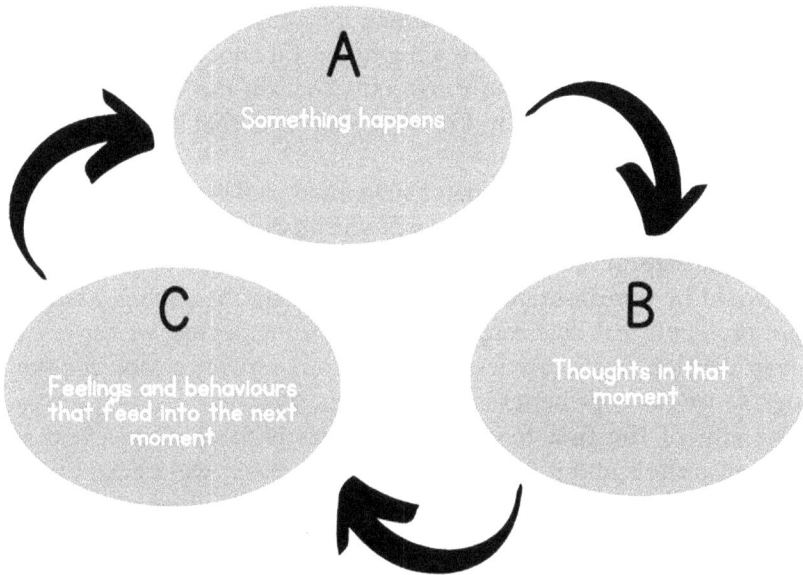

Our beliefs drive how we feel and behave in that moment, but they can also have a knock-on effect for the next. This is a self-fulfilling prophecy: once we believe something we will only notice things which support that. Carla's day is doomed because she believes it is doomed. We will see examples of this as we continue to build on the ABC skill.

Don't sweat the small stuff, or should we?

The small things are worth noticing, if not sweating. Often what we do is let them go. We say to ourselves:

- It doesn't really matter.
- It's not a big deal.
- I'm just going to ignore it.
- I'm going to bury it, push it under the carpet.

But what happens, in terms of our mental resilience, when those small things start to build up, in ever-increasing layers? This can happen if we ignore them; we think okay that doesn't matter, the kids only left their shoes there once. I've asked them not to, but no worries. Then I do something else. I go to the sink, and I notice they haven't washed up, but hey ho, don't sweat it. It's really not a big thing. I'll choose my battles. Then my husband walks in and he throws his coat on the chair, and I think, well, he's been at work all day, I'm not going to let that bother me. I'll just ignore it.

There are now three things that I've ignored, and if each is creating even a small reaction, then my resilience will start to drain away. One more thing and I might snap, because all those little things build up.

It would be unrealistic to ABC every issue, but by paying attention to minor problems that do create a reaction to some degree, we can use ABC to help develop our awareness and keep our resilience tank for the big things, so we can cope better in the moment.

The aim of the first four skills chapters is to develop a real sense of self-awareness about how we tend to act when we are experiencing certain emotions. This builds our emotional intelligence, helping us to understand ourselves. This can also build empathy for others; for example, although you might not feel angry in a particular situation, you do know what it feels like, and how you behave when you have that emotion, so you have more empathy when you see anger in someone else.

Summary

The ABC skill is super simple. We encourage you to start practising it with the small everyday things, to build self-awareness and understanding. Over time, you can apply it to bigger situations too. We have learnt that:

- The ABC helps us to be clear on the situation, the beliefs we have in the moment about that, and how we feel and behave.
- Our beliefs can create self-fulfilling prophecies. They drive how we feel and react and we can take those with us into the next moment, and round and round we go.

- It is also a great way to communicate as it's the basis of a new language framework, helping you to explain to yourself and others what is going on, at least from a personal perspective. Imagine your whole family knowing the principles and practice of the ABC, each of you being able to clearly explain what happened, the beliefs and feelings and behaviour.
- This clarity has the potential to keep lines of communication open through a shared understanding.

Activities for teenagers

Be thoughtful about when and how to share the activities with your youngsters. You know your teenager better than anyone, so you decide when and how to use them. The purpose of these activities is to teach them that there is a link between thoughts, feelings, and behaviour. These examples focus on *why* beliefs to keep it simple for you and them.

ABC practice one:
Complete the thought bubbles that would lead to the different feelings.

Activating Event	Beliefs Thoughts at the time	Consequence
A trip that Sahid was looking forward to has been cancelled		Feel Sad
A trip that Sahid was looking forward to has been cancelled		Feel Angry
A trip that Sahid was looking forward to has been cancelled		Feel Ok

ABC practice two:
This time have a go at completing both the beliefs and the consequences.

Activating Event	Beliefs Thoughts at the time	Consequence
Josh has lots of homework to finish tonight		
Leanne is not allowed to meet her friends because she needs to go the shops with her dad		
Melody has been sent to her room for arguing with her sister		

ABC practice three:
Think of some of your own: start with something good that happened and practise using ABC. Then choose two, small everyday situations that you didn't like so much, or didn't turn out so well, and left you feeling or behaving in a way that was unhelpful.

Activating Event	Beliefs Thoughts at the time	Consequence

Notes

1 Masten AS. (2019). Resilience from a Developmental Systems Perspective. *World Psychiatry*, 18, 101–102. https://doi.org/10.1002/wps.20591

2 Seligman M, Csikszentmihalyi M. (2000). An Introduction: Positive Psychology. *American Psychologist*. https://ppc.sas.upenn.edu/sites/default/files/ppintroarticle.pdf

Don't believe everything you think

5

Reframing with optimism

Now that we recognise that it's not what happens that leads to unhelpful consequences, it's what we believe to be true about it, we can see how important it is to think flexibly and realistically. If our thoughts are accurate, then we have choices. We can look for what we might have missed, we can think differently about it and take some control of the situation.

This is the skill of reframing. At its heart is our own self-awareness, our realisation that we are prone to have habits of thought.

We all need habits; they are useful shortcuts except when they obstruct us. Habits are basically our brains working efficiently. We need pathways in our thinking to help us through the day without questioning everything. The brain stores our past experiences to explain the causes of situations, to notice the unusual, and anticipate the future. Without that, we would literally need to question everything before any decisions or actions could be taken.

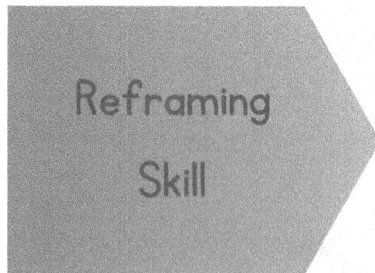

Reframing

Skill

DOI: 10.4324/9781003581994-6

Think about learning a foreign language, as we all did in our school days. A novice needs to think hard about every single aspect, starting with the simplest and most frequent words: yes and no; please and thank you. Later, we learn the common phrases for everyday exchanges: how are you? What's your name? Then more detailed conversation. All these layers must be memorised one at a time, until we are able to start combining them into sentences. Eventually the brain is working so efficiently that we can produce whole paragraphs automatically.

In a way we can think of the skills of psychological fitness as a kind of language that we are aiming to speak fluently. Once we have learned all the individual skills, we will experience the magic of combining the skills in many ways according to the situations we face.

As we can see, on the one hand our brain works efficiently, on the other it makes mistakes. We miss information because our habits mean that our thinking is biased. For example, if I struggled at school to learn a new language and someone suggests I try now, I might kick back and ignore the suggestion because I think: I tried that once and I was terrible, I won't be any better now and anyhow I don't want to look a fool. Our habit of thinking means we don't even give it a go; we dismiss the idea out of hand. We have several of these habits of thinking, we make assumptions based on our experience, we jump to conclusions based on what we believe to be true, and we lose perspective when we believe the worst will happen.

If we layer the knowledge of habits with our understanding of the link between what we think, how we feel, and how we behave, we can begin to see how unhelpful our habits can be.

We continue using our experience to influence our decisions rather than being open to different ideas. Now imagine if we have a habit of thinking about something more significant. Let's say we have a habit that tells us we don't deal well with change because we once struggled when we started a new job. We take one situation and create a habit of thinking that is unhelpful when we are faced with any type of change. This is where reframing has the capacity to help us to see the situation in a different way, from a new angle, and maybe see that change is not always difficult.

The skill of reframing begins with identifying our unhelpful habits and to do this we need to recognise them.

There are several common habits of thought, but as a starter let's focus on the three main ones, to demonstrate the reframing skill.

Me habit

This situation happened because of me. I internalise and think it was my responsibility, or I am to blame. Beliefs include:

- It's my fault
- They left because of something I said
- It wouldn't have happened if it wasn't for me
- They are too good for me
- My point of view isn't of value

Them habit

If it's not my fault it must be somebody else's: it's them. This is the opposite of the me habit. The reason something happened is because of somebody or something else external to me. Beliefs include:

- It's nothing to do with me
- They made me do this
- It's their responsibility
- I didn't do or say anything

Always habit

The reason the activating event happened is permanent. The way we think about the situation is unchangeable and fixed. Always beliefs include:

- That's just the way it is
- It's never going to change
- It's always like this
- They are lazy
- This is horrible

Now just stop for a moment and ask yourself: **what lasts forever? What is permanent?**

You may have thought about:

- The sun rising and setting every day – we certainly hope that continues to happen.
- Death being permanent – although not everyone believes death is finite, some people believe in reincarnation, for example.
- Plastic is permanent – yes, probably plastic is something that is very hard to get rid of; we know how difficult that is.

The point is that not many things last forever, are fixed, unchangeable.

Patterns of thinking

These patterns of thought: me, them, always, are habitual mistakes our brains make, by missing information about the situation. This limits our ability to see the whole picture. Let's look at some examples of what might be missing.

ME: explains events from an internal perspective, so it may miss information about the external factors. Who or what else might have contributed to the situation?

THEM: explains events from an external perspective – it may miss information about how I have contributed.

ALWAYS: these beliefs imply that the cause of a problem is permanent and unchanging. Words like always, never, forever, and just the way it is lead to a lack of action, and there is simply no point in trying.

Habits in our thinking can keep us stuck, making it harder to see things in a new way that might help us do something different, or to feel differently about a situation, or to see what's really going on. Sometimes staying stuck means we stay safe. Contining to take the same journey to work despite it taking me ten minutes longer each day means we don't have to get lost again, or to feel uncomfortable. The emotional payoff is worth it even though the longer route means rising earlier, taking an earlier train, rushing to take the children to breakfast club. These habits become engrained, but reframing offers potential to understand ourselves better, and deal more effectively with the world around us.

Imagine this

Pete let himself in the front door, feeling good. He enjoyed his job, and he'd had a particularly interesting day, with talk of a possible promotion coming up.

In the kitchen he hugged Carla. "How was your day?"

"Horrible," she said, "and exhausting."

"Anything I can do to help?" Pete asked.

"Yeah, you could clear the kitchen table, wash the dishes, tell the kids to stop leaving their bags everywhere, and buy some eggs."

"Phew," Pete said. "What's happened?"

"Ella drives me crazy sometimes. She takes me for granted and doesn't take responsibility– and we mollycoddle her and let her get away with it, but now she's going to be in trouble at school tomorrow and it's all my fault!" Carla sighed heavily.

Pete hugged her. "Let's sit down and talk about it."

"I feel terrible Pete, she's upset because I was so mean to her. I'm hopeless. I never remember anything."

"Well you do have a lot to juggle and you remember most things. I can't actually recall the last time you forgot anything."

"Well Ella asked me to buy eggs for cookery tomorrow, and I forgot, and now she is in trouble because of me."

"Ella is growing up, she could have checked yesterday and reminded you."

"True, but I do usually do it all for her, so it is my fault."

"We're both guilty of that Carla. This is a good lesson for Ella, to realise you're not Superwoman. Look this is good for us, we need to help her grow up and take more responsibility."

Pete called Ella to come downstairs.

She appeared sheepish. "What have I done now?"

Pete said, "I hear things were a bit heated tonight."

Carla said, "I'm sorry for shouting at you Ella. I totally forgot about the eggs and felt bad and that made me snap at you. The thing is I have lots to remember, and you are growing up and maybe you could help me more. What do you think? Could you have done anything different about the eggs?"

"I should have mentioned it yesterday, but to be honest I forgot I had cooking. I was thinking could we pop out to the corner shop and get some."

Pete said, "That sounds like a plan." He winked at Carla. "Shall I pick up fish and chips on the way back, save cooking tonight?"

The process for reframing

The route to flexible and realistic reframing goes like this:

- You're in a situation where the way you are feeling and/or behaving is unhelpful
- ABC the situation

Carla's beliefs at the time	Code the habits	Reframing after using the questions
We mollycoddle her.	• Always	Carla and Pete can change how they help Ella grow up.
She takes me for granted.	• Them	Both Pete and Carla are guilty of doing everything for Ella.
She should do more for herself at her age.	• Them	Carla does normally do it all for Ella.
I'm hopeless.	• Me & Always	Carla remembers most things and she has a lot to juggle.

- Me: How did others or circumstance contribute here?
- Them: How did I contribute, or what would have been in my control?
- Always: How long will this last, what is changeable?

- Look at the beliefs and code them: is that a me, them, or always belief?
- Ask yourself some questions to help you see the potential to reframe what you think has happened, for example:
  - Me: How did others or circumstance contribute here?
  - Them: How did I contribute, or what would have been in my control?
  - Always: How long will this last, what is changeable?

Listening with empathy

Reframing helps us to find what is really going on at a personal level. By understanding that beliefs drive the consequences of feelings and behaviour, our empathy develops our potential to listen deeply to others. If we understand that we have habits of thinking, then this opens us up to recognise that in others, and then we have more empathy for them.

The aim is not to fix problems for others, but rather to listen in a different way to understand what the problem is, which may not be obvious. Focusing on the beliefs, rather than what has happened, provides a different way of supporting our children with the unhelpful feelings they have or the way they are behaving. Once we tune in to the beliefs, we can empathise. Because we understand what it feels like to feel sad, or angry, or embarrassed, we are more tuned into the potential for habits of thought. We might not want them to feel sad, or to behave in an angry way, but we can understand their reactions, and the situation, at a deeper level.

Summary

Reframing is the next step of mental resilience, offering us a way of understanding ourselves. That enables us to be effective in dealing with difficult moments and prevents us from being stuck with unrealistic and unhelpful thoughts. We have learnt that:

- Our brains work efficiently creating thought habits, but that means we can miss important information.
- Some common habits include me, them, and always beliefs that can obstruct us and lead to unhelpful feelings and behaviours.
- If we identify our thinking habits, we can use questions to help complete the picture.
- Once we can see the situation more accurately and realistically, there is potential to create new ideas about how to approach the problem.
- As we tune into our habits, we build empathy, helping us to understand ourselves and relate to others better.

Activities for teenagers

The purpose of these activities is to introduce the idea of habits in thinking that we all have and that sometimes they can get in the way, like a gremlin. Use them to teach this to your teenagers. Don't try and change what they think; the aim here is for them to understand the component parts and the value of reframing.

Introduce these two characters:

Jesse can see the good things in life. She doesn't think everything is rosy and good all the time, but when faced with difficult situations she is able to be positive and hopeful about her life. She is optimistic.

Jayden tends to see the bad in a situation. When something good happens, he doesn't enjoy it because he can only think about when it will end. He has a negative and gloomy outlook. He is pessimistic.

Activity Jesse and Jayden have been invited to Mo's party, a friend from their class. It has been postponed as Mo's mum is not well.

- How will Jesse react and what will she say to Mo?
- How will Jayden react and what will he say to Mo?
- Who would you rather be friends with and why?
- If Jayden were your friend, and you wanted to stay friends with him, how could you help him to be more optimistic?

As an alternative, suggest to your child that they write a story about the occasion.

Meet the Gremlin Beliefs
Read the descriptions.

Meet the Gremlin Beliefs		
ME Gremlin Beliefs	THEM Gremlin Beliefs	Always Gremlin Beliefs
Me Gremlin Beliefs focus on the situation being caused by me. The reason why something has happened is completely my fault or my responsibility. This Gremlin overlooks how other people or circumstances may have contributed.	Them Gremlin Beliefs focus on the situation being caused by other people or something else. The situation has been caused by something external to me, out there. This Gremlin overlooks my contribution to the situation or the things that could be in my control.	Always Gremlin Beliefs focus on things lasting forever. The reason why something has happened is true and is going to be true forever. This Gremlin makes things seem hopeless. If the situation is true and is going to last forever then what is the point? I might as well not try and/or give up.

ACTIVITY
Write or draw an image of the three gremlins as headings on a blank piece of paper.

- Me Gremlin Beliefs
- Them Gremlin Beliefs
- Always Gremlin Beliefs

Gremlin Belief Cards

Everything is just terrible	My friend didn't keep the promise they made	They are selfish	I've got a spot on my face, I'm pure ugly	It's not worth the effort
Mum is a nag in the morning	Asking for help is a weakness	I'll make everyone feel worse if I tell them how I am feeling	I failed in Geography and let myself down	They left me out of the group chat on purpose
My hair is a mess, I look awful	The teacher hates me	That test didn't go well, I got everything wrong	My parents put too much pressure on me	He didn't laugh at my joke, what an idiot he is
There is no point in learning anything in school	People at school are really unfriendly	It wouldn't have happened if I hadn't been there	Teachers don't understand	There is no point in learning anything in school
What I do doesn't make any difference to anyone else	I said the wrong thing again	Nobody takes me seriously	They make me look stupid	What I do doesn't make any difference to anyone else

Print and cut up or write on your own cards.

Sort the Gremlin Beliefs Cards.

Sort the cards under the Gremlin pictures.

Choose five Gremlin Belief Cards and write a few sentences about how these beliefs might be helpful or hindering to someone and explain why.

Why did I react that way? Identifying what matters most   **6**

Sometimes, our thoughts and feelings are driven by our deepest values, often outside our conscious awareness. These are big sticky beliefs, and we can spot when they are activated because the way we react doesn't make sense to us, so we need to search a little deeper.

We know there is a direct link between beliefs, feelings, and behaviour, and, so far, we have been developing our understanding about in-the-moment beliefs, what we think right then and there, and how those thoughts drive how we feel and behave at the time.

These in-the-moment beliefs are informed by our perspective of what has happened to us, and this can change depending on what is going on around us. For example, if you are feeling unwell, and you have an important and busy day, you might think: my life is tough; that makes sense to us. It is not necessarily completely true, but you understand why you had thought like that: because you were unwell and had a busy day ahead, and that was bothering you. But sometimes what has happened, and the thoughts you

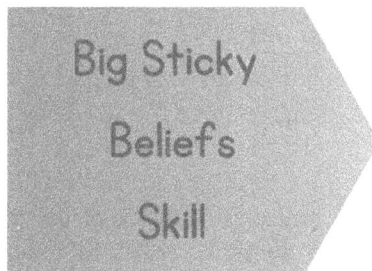

Big Sticky

Beliefs

Skill

DOI: 10.4324/9781003581994-7

have about it, are not so obviously linked, so we might need to search a little deeper, beyond our in-the-moment beliefs, to see the true picture.

Something to try

Finish the sentences with your first ideas . . .
- The world is . . .
- People are . . .
- Children should . . .

The way we finish these sentences will depend on many things, including our upbringing, our environment, our experiences, and what we know to be true. Also, our values, which are the BIG ideas we have about how the world should be, the rights and wrongs of situations. Global ideas – for example, people should be kind, not just in some contexts but always – will apply across many situations, some of them conscious, some of them totally out of our awareness.

Big sticky beliefs

Mostly we are aware of these BIG, value-based beliefs. For example, if we value the idea that people should be kind and we see somebody being unkind, we might think:

- that person hasn't been brought up correctly
- they don't know how to behave

and that might lead to us to feel angry and say something to them, for example: you shouldn't behave like that.

When this happens it's clear that we have a BIG value belief informing how we think in the moment.

Big because they are beliefs about how the world should be, how people should behave, and why things happen the way they do.

Sticky because they tend to be global. We don't just think people should be kind in certain situations; we think they should be kind always.

These beliefs are so big and sticky that we perceive them as the truth. We forget they are just the way we think, and sometimes we don't realise they are in play, informing and driving how we feel and behave.

Because they are big and sticky we perceive them as the truth, so we are not always aware that they are informing, and even sometimes overriding, our in-the-moment beliefs.

Understanding what really matters to me

There are a few ways to notice whether big sticky beliefs are active in a situation, for example:

- Our reaction to the activating event is out of proportion to what's happened.
- Our consequences don't make any sense to us. Our in-the-moment beliefs should lead us to feel angry, but we feel something quite different.
- There is a disconnect between what we think and how we feel and behave.
- We just can't make our minds up. We might have thought about it and spoken to somebody else, but we cannot decide what to do.

If any of these things are true it might be a big sticky belief, in play, but out of your awareness.

Imagine this

Carla felt strongly that water was a precious resource and that everyone should play their part in preserving water and certainly not wasting it. Her family all knew this. She had asked them to do simple things such as not overfilling the kettle, turning off the tap whilst brushing their teeth, and using a water butt in the garden.

Activating Event: it's early evening and Carla walked into the kitchen. Joe was standing at the sink chatting to Pete, who was laughing. Behind him the kitchen tap was on full blast. The kettle was whistling, full to the top, with Pete's one cup in front of it.

Carla's in-the-moment **Beliefs**:

- I shouldn't bother; it's a waste of time.
- They deliberately ignore me.
- They are all selfish.
- Pete's the worst, he should know better. He undermines me.

Consequences: Carla shouted, "You all make me sick to my stomach!" She continued shouting as she slammed the kitchen door, stormed upstairs, slammed the bedroom door, sat on her bed, and wept. She felt a deep sense of sadness and began to cry uncontrollably. She knew she ought to meditate or write in her journal to manage the emotions that were overwhelming her, but she simply couldn't raise the energy. She stayed in her room and didn't talk to anyone all night even when Pete came to bed later.

Let's unpick Carla's situation.

- Was the way Carla felt, and how she behaved, helping or hindering her? She was now sitting alone in her bedroom, unable to speak to anyone, and extremely upset, so we'd say hindering.
- Was the way she felt and behaved going to help her family make any changes to their behaviour around water? Her family were a bit in shock. They didn't know what had caused this, it had nothing to do with them, and they didn't know how to help her. They weren't sure what to think.
- Was Carla's reaction in proportion to the situation or an overreaction? Her reaction seemed, on face value, out of proportion. All that had happened was that the kitchen tap was running, and the kettle was full, and her family were happily unaware of both.

If Carla kept telling her family to do something and they kept ignoring it, then a big reaction might well be needed, but the point here is that Carla had a BIG reaction and the way she was feeling and behaving just didn't match her beliefs.

Her feelings that her family were all deliberately ignoring her, and they were all selfish, would make more sense if they led to Carla feeling angry, standing her ground, and making sure they all knew that she was disappointed by their behaviour. So, storming off, crying deeply, and not talking to anybody all night, that seemed odd. There was a disconnect between Carla's beliefs and her consequences and her reaction to the activating event did seem out of proportion. Something else was happening that she was unaware of, that resulted in her storming off and feeling sad all evening.

Maybe there was a big sticky belief in play informing this situation. But how could Carla identify what else might be going on here other than her in-the-moment beliefs? How could she work out what was really driving her reaction?

Ask *what*, not *why*

The skill is to slow things down and use specific questions, to reflect on what was going on. Carla needed to ask herself *what* mattered most, not *why* it happened.

When we ask **why** we reacted like that, we are more likely to defend ourselves by reinforcing all the reasons why:

- because they're horrible
- they don't listen to me
- they don't respect me
- my point of view doesn't matter

What questions force us to look deeper, to reflect, and to really think about what was happening.

- **What** was the most upsetting part of that for me?
- **What** was the worst part of that for me?
- **What** does that mean to me?

Carla used the *what* questions to bring her deeper thoughts into awareness:

- **What** is the most upsetting part of that for me?
  Pete knows that saving water is important to me.
- **What** is the worst part of that for me?
  He doesn't care about or value what is important to me.
- **What** does that mean to me?
  Couples that last care and value the same things, and our relationship is different to this.

The reason Carla was sitting upstairs crying was because she felt she had lost something in her relationship with Pete. She thought their relationship was one thing and actually it was something else. Carla's BIG sticky belief was *couples that last care for and value the same things. But she and Pete didn't.*

That belief was overriding her in-the-moment beliefs and driving the way she felt and behaved. Now that Carla was aware of that, she had choices.

What Carla did next

Initially she didn't do anything at all. Her deep dive into her reactions had given her a new understanding, and that made her feel better. She realised that her feelings weren't necessarily out of proportion, because in that moment she thought there was something wrong with her relationship with Pete, so no wonder she was sitting upstairs sobbing. This had nothing to do with water, or taps, or kettles. It was about her belief that the situation had challenged her relationship, and that made her feel profoundly sad.

Carla sat on it for a few days. She played around in her head with her new awareness, asking herself: do I want to reinforce this belief or is there something I could do to take more control of it, perhaps change it? She thought perhaps she could have a conversation with Pete about this, rather than about water and whether he supports her with the kids or not. So, she planned an evening with Pete, when they would have time for each other, with the children in bed and out of earshot.

"Look Pete, you know that conserving water is really important to me. It's obviously not so important to you and that worries me. I think that couples that stay happily together need to care about and value the same things. You don't care about water in the same way that I do and that's why I was so upset the other day because I'm worried that our relationship is fragile."

Pete frowned. "Blimey love, I honestly didn't make that connection at all, and I'm not sure I agree with you. We are individuals as well as a couple. I like things that you don't and vice versa. I would say that makes our relationship richer and stronger, not weaker."

"But Pete, water conservation is really important to me, and I want the kids to do their bit to look after it. It's a big thing for me, and if you don't care about it, that's a problem."

"I see," Pete said. "I mean I really do see that, and I am sorry. I can't say that I am always going to be a hundred percent right, but you have helped me see that it is more important to you than I had realised. You mean so much to me, you are my wife, my friend, my teacher." He smiled at her. "I will try harder."

> ***Having the right conversation meant Carla and Pete understood each other better.***

Using the *what* questions is a powerful way to understand what is really going on beneath the surface. In this respect, they are a reflective tool, encouraging us to think inwardly, bringing into our awareness how our value-based beliefs can drive our everyday reactions.

With our partners, adult friends, and work colleagues who seem stuck, we can explain the *what* questions and show how they clarify difficult situations, by describing:

- the activating event, what exactly happened
- what they thought about it at the time
- how they felt and behaved at the time

Then we can pick one or two *what* questions to help them focus in on the issues.

It is vital that we stop the discussion when they feel they have understood something useful.

We are focusing in here on value-based beliefs, and that's fragile territory for others to tread. Our role as a friend is to ask the questions, not probe for answers. If we think about Carla's situation, she came to understand that she thought her relationship was in trouble, a hard place to explore with others. So, what we don't want to do is push someone further than they want to explore, or dig too deep, out of our own fascination or desire to help. This means that the question: what does that mean to you? might be one you leave with them to think about on their own, as Carla did, to mull it over before thinking about what to do next.

Imagine this

Pete was home first from work and opened a letter from the school saying their son Joe had received a detention for being rude to a teacher. Pete and/ or Carla were asked to attend a meeting with the head teacher and Joe, the following day.

Pete felt furious and his immediate urge was to call Joe back from his after-school football practice. Then he paused, thinking: Joe will shut down if I shout at him and that won't help me understand what has happened here. He is not usually rude to teachers, and I need to know the facts for everyone's sake.

When Joe arrived home, Pete asked him what had happened.

"That teacher has it in for me," Joe said. "She always has, she hates me and tries to embarrass me in front of everyone. I hate her."

"Ok Joe, message received. I want to support you the best way I can at school tomorrow. What did she do to embarrass you?"

"She asked me a question that I couldn't answer, in front of everyone." Joe said.

"What was the most upsetting part of that for you?" Pete asked,

Joe looked at his dad, puzzled, and said "What, that I didn't know the answer?"

"Yes," Pete said. "What was the worst part of that for you?"

"I looked a right idiot. The girls sniggered because it was a question I should have been able to answer."

Pete replied, "I totally understand how it feels to be embarrassed in front of your friends. But teachers are there to ask questions and the school don't usually invite us in, so they must think it's important. Can you explain the being rude part?"

Joe grimaced. "I told her she was a rubbish teacher and that I hate maths because of her."

Pete gulped inside, but instead of telling Joe off he asked, "What can I do to help?"

"There's not really anything you can do Dad. I've been rude, I've got a detention."

Pete asked, "What can you do to help yourself then, to try and change things for the better? After all she is going to be your maths teacher unless you want to ask for a different one, if that's an option?"

"Well, I can be honest tomorrow and tell her I'm sorry for being rude."

"Does she know you were embarrassed for not knowing the answer?"

"No because I just clammed up when she kept me behind."

"Maybe you could include that tomorrow, so she understands the reason behind you being rude," Pete suggested.

"I suppose so," Joe said. "I don't want to move maths classes because that will make things worse."

"It's a good lesson for you," Pete said. "She won't be the first person in your life that you don't get on with or have to work with. It's helpful to try and channel your personal views into what you want to achieve, in this case a maths GCSE, and take the attention away from you. If you manage that I'll be even more proud of you than I am already."

This isn't about fudging the rules. Being rude to teachers is not acceptable, and will result in being in trouble, but by using *what* questions Pete not only understood what had happened, he also kept the lines of communication open and dealt with the situation as effectively as he could, taking the sting out of it as much as possible. Joe still had a detention to do. They still had a meeting with the head teacher to contend with, but they hopefully learned from understanding what had happened. Joe will learn a useful life lesson with his father's supportive approach.

Summary

When we overreact to a situation, or the way we have responded doesn't make any sense, we need to think beyond our immediate beliefs and dig deeper into our thoughts and feelings. We have learnt that:

- Asking *what* questions helps us to focus inwards on what matters for us.
- It's helpful to give ourselves time to reflect on our new awareness before deciding what to do next.

- Ask *what* rather than *why* questions to keep lines of communication open with your teenagers and understand what matters to them.
- Don't press them for answers or problem solutions; simply leave them to think about matters in their own time.

Activities for teenagers

The *what* questions can be useful when our teenagers can't articulate their worries and concerns. Rather than using them as we would with adults, they can be a helpful way to help them to focus and reflect inward, to bring out what they are thinking, zooming in on what really matters to them at a personal level.

Using *what* instead of *why* also means we keep lines of communication open; our teenagers are less likely to feel judged when we ask, what matters most to you about that? When we ask what does that mean to you? We are inadvertently telling them we care about what matters to them, we are willing to listen to them. The purpose is to help them understand what is going on for them. Don't use *what* questions as a way to seek an answer, but as a tool to help them reflect and focus in on what matters most to them.

You are teaching your children to think about what is important to them.

Where the superpowers begin

7

So far, the main use of the skills has been to develop self-awareness about how you think, feel, and behave, to understand what gets in the way. We are sure there will have been light bulb moments when you have recognised a habit or identified a big sticky belief. You may well have felt guilty about the way you have reacted or behaved or both. If this is the case, feel proud. It is an achievement to notice what needs to change. It's brave to be willing to look inward, to do the self-awareness work; it shows you care.

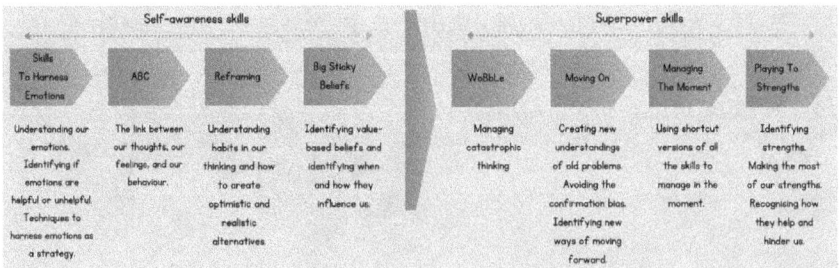

Self-awareness skills					Superpower skills			
Skills To Harness Emotions	ABC	Reframing	Big Sticky Beliefs		WoBbLe	Moving On	Managing The Moment	Playing To Strengths
Understanding our emotions. Identifying if emotions are helpful or unhelpful. Techniques to harness emotions as a strategy.	The link between our thoughts, our feelings, and our behaviour.	Understanding habits in our thinking and how to create optimistic and realistic alternatives.	Identifying value-based beliefs and identifying when and how they influence us.		Managing catastrophic thinking	Creating new understandings of old problems. Avoiding the confirmation bias. Identifying new ways of moving forward.	Using shortcut versions of all the skills to manage in the moment.	Identifying strengths. Making the most of our strengths. Recognising how they help and hinder us.

Now we want to shift the focus to helping you make changes, to be able to keep things in perspective rather than catastrophise, and to move on from unhelpful thinking. But before we delve into these new skills, let's consider some important distinctions that underpin the use of the four superpowers.

DOI: 10.4324/9781003581994-8

The difference between self-efficacy[1] and self-esteem

There are several terms that describe how we think about ourselves. As well as self-efficacy and self-esteem which we are focusing on here, there are other related terms:

- Self-confidence, which is a positive attitude about our skills and abilities.
- Self-belief, which is a global sense of yourself as a person.
- Self-acceptance, which is to be at peace with yourself.

A strong sense of self-efficacy promotes human accomplishment and personal well-being, and the ability to face challenges as something to be mastered rather than threats to avoid. People with high self-efficacy can recover from failure faster. To develop this capacity, we need to both understand the skills, and believe in ourselves and our ability.

Self-efficacy is different from self-esteem, because it's tangible: we can feel it, see it, hear it, and we can't have too much of it.

Self-esteem is how we think about ourselves, our self-opinion. When something knocks it, we are not really sure why. Too much self-esteem is entirely possible, as some influencers on social media demonstrate daily with a certain arrogance or air of superiority. It's also possible to have too little self-esteem, or self-respect, which often leads to a lack of self-confidence.

Self-efficacy is a skill, a strategy that I know and trust, that will help me through difficult times, despite my self-esteem being dented sometimes.

High levels of self-efficacy can be recognised when one or more of the following statements is true for someone faced with a setback or challenge:

- **Mastery of the skills:** I believe I can do this because I have learnt through doing something similar before.
- **An accessible role model:** I know someone who is a bit like me that has been able to do this.
- **Social connection and mastery combined:** I have talked this through with someone and I have a strategy that I think will work.
- **Emotional state and realistic capability:** I am calm, and physically able to do what is needed.

Skills are an essential building block for self-efficacy because they provide the opportunity to learn and understand something concrete.

Practicing the skills enough for them to be mastered is the know-how we talked about earlier. It's the difference between someone saying: don't let that bother you, it's not worth stewing about, ignore it. Versus: when things like that bother me, I try this . . . and it works like this. . . . Do you think that could be helpful for you? Is it worth a try?

This small yet powerful change of language has an enabling power, encouraging without judgement, offering a tangible solution, and with the detail on how to use it. Skills create opportunities to talk through ways of dealing with difficulty with a shared language and approach that can be replicated, mastered, and tweaked for use in different situations. Creating the capacity for self-belief must be grounded in the reality that we can be effective.

The difference between empathy and sympathy

The learning of skills is connected to empathy, which helps us to focus on solutions rather than dwelling on the situation or ignoring it. We can express that we feel sorry for someone, that we have sympathy for the person, but that can sometimes be hard to absorb, as it's a transaction from one person to another, but without a shared emotional connection. Often, we express our sympathy to others by starting with "at least":

- Josh is in trouble at school again, but *at least* he is an A star student.
- It's tough but *at least* it won't last long.
- You've had a miscarriage but *at least* you know you can get pregnant.
- Your relationship has failed but *at least* you don't have to put up with their moaning.

When we express sympathy, we feel pity for the other person, and we are trying to make them feel better.

Empathy is the willingness and ability to step in and feel with others.[2]

Empathy is different: we know what it feels like to experience that emotion. It evokes a feeling in us, it often takes more thought, and it requires connection to the other person. It might sound like this:

- I spoke to the school pastoral lead when my son had a bad year, I can come with you if it would help.
- I understand that it is tough for you right now, what do you need?

- I don't know what to say right now, I am glad you felt able to tell me, and I am here for you.

This takes vulnerability because it requires an awareness of what it feels like to experience emotion, to have been in a situation that may be comparable or similar and then transferring that understanding into this situation for them.

Empathy is not saying: Oh, I know what that feels like because when this happened to me . . . and then hijacking the conversation to talk about our situation. That is more like sympathy, often used to avoid the other person's emotions.

> *This can be particularly true when it comes to confronting the difficult emotions of our teenagers.*

We don't want them to feel down, or upset, of course we don't: but we need to acknowledge where they are, allow them space, and recognise that we can't always make things better for them. It's often better to simply say to our teenage children: *I am just so glad you told me.*

When we jump in and try and repair the situation, we are sending them a message: You can't deal with this. When we undermine the importance of something they are facing by saying: Don't worry about that, it will all be forgotten by next week, we are sending them a message that says their situation is irrelevant.

> *A sympathetic response is more likely to close down conversation, whereas an empathetic response keeps lines of communication open.*

Figure 7.2 helps us to listen with empathy to our teenagers. On the left are the consequences and on the right is a summary headline of beliefs.

For example, They've lost something important to them could be that they are thinking:

- My friend doesn't like me anymore
- It will never be the same

Something bad or dangerous could be that they are thinking:

- It's my job to look out for them
- They are disrespecting my family

Listening with empathy

If you see or hear:	The beliefs sit within this heading
They are sad or withdrawing	They have lost something important to them
They are anxious or agitated	Something bad or dangerous is happening
They are angry or aggressive	Something is wrong and is causing harm
They are feeling guilty or trying to make amends	Their actions have caused harm
They feel or act embarrassed	They do not meet the standard they believe is expected

Figure 7.2

The ability to empathise, to belong, and to love is at the heart of the capacity to form and create human connections and to develop and sustain relationships. Our teenagers want us as their parents to think they are doing a good job. We would go further and say that most of us want other people to think they are essentially good people. Most people *are* good, trying to get on with their lives in the best way possible.

The difference between general praise and process praise[3]

When our children are small, we encourage them, we tell them that they are amazing and wonderful, that they drew the best drawing ever. It feels good for us and them.

As they grow up, we generally stop being so vocal about what is going well. We focus in on what is going wrong, what needs to improve or change. We all respond to praise: no matter how old we are, we all love to know what we are doing well.

We remember criticism, but we respond to praise.

Think for a moment about what happens when we criticise another person, in a work situation for example. We think carefully about what we will say and consider how it will sound to the other person and how they might receive it.

Yet when we praise, we often do it without too much thought. You are amazing, wonderful, you did great. It might feel good to hear praise like this in the moment, but it is not that helpful beyond the moment.

Why? Because I don't know *why* I am amazing and wonderful. Although I like the idea that others think I am great, it might encourage me to stay away from them because if I stay too close, they might see that I am actually not that amazing after all.

Imagine that your child brings home a drawing from school, and you say: Wow, that's a wonderful picture, I'm going to put it on the fridge. Your child feels good because you like their drawing, but the opportunity to grow their potential with your praise has been missed because you have not told them *why* you like the picture.

Process praise focuses on why the picture is good: I love your drawing because of the bright colours you used, and because you included windows and doors and a roof. Your child still feels good, and they know *why* you think it's good.

This specific way of framing praise encourages connection and growth, so we need to continue to use it as our children move through adolescence and into adulthood. Process praise is meaningful and helpful, as it comes with evidence that is hard to dispute and prevents our teenagers saying: well, you would say that because you are my mum/dad, but it's not true.

Unless we are thoughtful about the way in which we praise, it becomes white noise, empty words that can be quickly ignored. Process praise comes with evidence so it is much harder to ignore.

Imagine this

Carla encouraged her children in everything they did. She was always telling them how great they were, how smart, that they could do anything they put their mind to.

Joe had an assignment to complete for GCSE coursework. Carla asked him how it was going.

"I'm worried Mum. I don't think it's good enough," Joe tutted and shook his head.

"Of course it is," Carla said. "You'll be brilliant, I know you will."

"You would say that," Joe replied and walked out. His mum's words were no comfort.

If Carla had taken the time to ask Joe what he was most worried about and then used some process praise based on a previous time when he had done better than he thought he would, her words would have been more useful to Joe.

For example, it could have gone like this:

Carla asked Joe how the GCSE coursework was going.

"I'm worried Mum. I don't think it's good enough," Joe tutted and shook his head.

"I can see how hard you have been working. Is there a particular bit that is a sticking point for you?" Carla asked.

"There's a bit in the middle that just isn't working right, and I don't know how to fix it," Joe replied.

"I remember hearing you practise presenting the information out loud for another piece of work, have you tried that on this yet?" Carla reminded him. "I remember thinking what a great tactic it was. I actually used it when I was presenting at work."

"Oh, I totally forgot that mum. Yeah, it's a great way to hear how it sounds, and work out what needs to change. Thanks, mum."

The difference between optimism and pessimism

Being resilient is not about turning negative situations into positive ones. Choosing the positive way of seeing something won't make difficulties disappear. Pretending the sky is blue and clear when it is grey and cloudy is unhelpful for dealing with the grey cloudiness.

Realistic thinking is very different to positive thinking; it's about the ability to notice the good things. It's the capacity to be optimistic.

Optimism is a choice that can be nurtured. It's the ability to focus on the good whilst not ignoring the bad. If we have a choice, and we usually do, taking the optimistic option will be more likely to move us forward – we're thinking: It's going to be hard, but I am not alone. Pessimism, on the other hand, can lead us to give up: I can't do this, it's too hard and no one will help.

Like any muscle, optimism needs to be nourished and nurtured. The more we notice the possibilities, the more we open our eyes and minds to them. Making an active choice to choose the new version of events is a positive step forward in developing that muscle.

Keeping lines of communication open

As our children grow, it is easy to fall into a cycle of nagging and reminding, partly because we are fixed in our thinking about our role as parents, and changes in what our teenagers need from us. As they develop, they need different things. If they are talking to us, coming to us for guidance and willing to listen, then we are in a good place.

It may be that lines of communication have broken down. In that case we can use our newfound skills to help us think about some of the reasons why that might be.

Communication can break down when:

- One person's Consequence is another person's Activating Event. The way our teenagers are feeling and behaving is an activating event for us. In this case we stop focusing on their needs, as we are drawn in, and fixate on how they are making us feel. We forget that it is not them making us feel that way, but rather our own beliefs about the way they are feeling. For example,
  - It is my fault my child is anxious. That leads to feeling guilty and trying to repair the damage we have caused.
  - I have taught them not to behave like that; they are showing me up. That leads to me feeling embarrassed, leaving the party early and avoiding future social events.
- We stop listening to each other with empathy. We talk to make our point, rather than truly listening and standing in their shoes. We forget what it is like to be young, that we are not walking their path, or we undermine what has happened to them.
- Our thinking is inaccurate and fixed, and we are not open and curious to the perspective of others. We have parented in a particular way because we read it somewhere or it is what our parents passed down, or what worked when they were young. We are not seeing that their world is different, that they are older, and that their needs have changed and therefore our parenting needs to adapt.
- Maybe our children do not live up to our ideals. For example, we teach our children manners, and then we are out, and they don't say please and thank you. That's mortifying because they are making you look like a bad parent, so you feel angry and tell them you are never taking them to a party again.

Keeping lines of communication open with our teenagers is vital. There are some simple things that you can have in mind that can help show them you care, that you are listening, and that you value them. For example:

- Be interested in what brings them joy.
- Be in the moment with them and truly listen. Put down whatever else it is you are doing and give them your full attention.
- Avoid early jump-ins when they are talking. Let them tell their story.
- Be genuine and authentic. It's fine to say: I don't really understand the fun in video games, but I love that it brings you joy, tell me about it.

- Ask questions to understand before offering advice.
- Ask about things that matter to them; give them chances to relive the things that matter most to them.

Effective communication is essential for human connections and for change. Not being able to express oneself in a calm, clear, and confident way can mean we become disconnected, give up, and feel that we are not able to make a difference.

There are different styles of communication: passive, aggressive, and assertive, and each can be helpful or unhelpful depending on what we wish the outcome to be.

Communication Styles		
Passive	Aggressive	Assertive
Avoids expressing opinions or feelings either verbally or nonverbally.	Expresses opinions and feelings forcefully in a manner that is verbally and/or physically abusive.	Expresses opinions and feelings in a clear, calm, and confident way.
This style might be exhibited with soft, low voices or not speaking at all. No eye contact. Slumped body posture.	This style might be exhibited with shouting, insulting words. Interrupting others, impulsive and reactive.	This style might be exhibited with a confident voice, good eye contact. Speaking with control and respect for others.
This style might be helpful when someone is happy to let others lead. The situation isn't really that important to them. Not stoking an argument while letting others vent.	This style might be helpful when decisive action is needed, for example in an emergency. To make a stand for the things they believe to be right. Protecting others.	This style might be helpful when someone needs to clearly express their views in a way that is respectful of others and themselves. When they want to take control of what is happening in a fair and controlled way.
This style might be unhelpful if someone doesn't feel able to speak and lets the situation build up until they explode or get ill. When someone is being mistreated but is too afraid to speak up.	This style might be unhelpful as it can generate fear. Come across as threatening, rude, disrespectful and so will push people away. Leads to aggressive behaviour and outbursts.	This style might be unhelpful if it means someone does not act quickly enough in an emergency, for example, where an aggressive style might be needed.

(Continued)

Continued

Communication Styles		
Passive	*Aggressive*	*Assertive*
Beliefs that could drive this style:	Beliefs that could drive this style:	Beliefs that could drive this style:
I do not have anything of value to say.	This is my responsibility. If I don't act no one will. If I don't show I am tough they will think I am weak.	I respect myself and others.
I don't really care about this.		I will get a better outcome if they understand what I am saying.
I'm frightened about what might happen.		We are equal.

Communication technique

Next is a tried and tested technique that can be useful when you need to communicate in a way that allows the other person to understand and hear what you are saying. In these situations, communicating in a calm, confident, and assertive style is going to be most effective.

- **Step 1: Describe the problem**
  As with the A in the ABC, describe just the facts. Who, what, where, and when. Do not exaggerate and do not include blame.
- **Step 2: Explain the reasons it is a problem**
  Own how you feel, use I statements: when this happens, I feel . . . Remember that your feelings are driven by your beliefs, so you may need to check for any habits of thinking and use the reframing or moving-on skill here before moving on to step 3. At step 2, reflect on how the change will affect them.
- **Step 3: Ask for a clear and fair change**
  Include what you will do, as well as what you would like the other person to change.
- **Step 4: Explain how the change will help**
  Include the benefits and the reasons it is reasonable for them as well as for you. Be prepared and open to negotiating at this step.

Communication is a two-way exchange and it requires both parties to listen to each other. Mostly what we tend to do when others are talking is prepare our answer. When we have something important to discuss it's worth taking time to think about what and how you say what you want to say. It's worth letting the other person know this is important to you, and that you have spent time thinking about how you will talk to them.

Use the four-step technique to help form the words, then practise saying them out loud to yourself, perhaps into a mirror until they feel authentic for you.

Imagine this

Ella had been given a score in an important mock exam, and it was much lower than she was expecting. She had checked her answers and compared them with a friend, and she felt the teacher had made an error. She needed to be clear and respectful; this was her teacher after all.

She asked for a time to talk to her teacher. It went like this:

"Thank you for meeting me. I have received my mock exam result back and I have a lower score than I was expecting. I worked hard on the paper, and I feel confused about why I have not done as well this time. As it is so important I did compare my answers with Mia, but I am still confused.

"I would be grateful if you could take another look to double check there has not been a mistake. I can ask Mia to give you her paper back too if it helps.

"I realise this is more work for you, and I may be missing something, but I would like to understand where I have gone wrong here so that I can prepare better for the actual exam. Would that be ok with you?"

This style of communication is clear, calm, confident, and respectful on all sides.

Summary

Up until now we have been learning the foundational self-awareness skills. The next chapter is where the superpowers begin. The focus shifts to helping you make changes. We considered some important distinctions that underpin the use of the four superpowers. We have learnt about:

- The difference between self-efficacy and self-esteem
- The difference between empathy and sympathy
- The difference between process praise and general praise
- The difference between optimism and pessimism
- How to keep lines of communication open

Communication activity for teenagers

Communication is such an important skill for young people and you will be supporting your teenagers to build their communication skills through learning the skills, creating the opportunity to build self-awareness that means they can articulate clearly what is going on for them. We also invite you to share this communication technique with them.

Communication Styles

Think about and answer the questions in the table about different communication styles

Passive	Aggressive	Assertive
Individuals avoid expressing their opinions or feelings.	Individuals express their opinions and feelings in a way that is verbally and/or physically abusive.	Individuals clearly state their views and feelings in a clear, calm, and confident way that values themselves and other people.
When is a passive communication style helpful?	When is an aggressive communication style helpful?	When is an assertive communication style helpful?
When is a passive communication style unhelpful?	When is an aggressive communication style unhelpful?	When is an assertive communication style unhelpful?
What might someone think if they choose to communicate passively?	What might someone think if they choose to communicate aggressively?	What might someone think if they choose to communicate assertively?
What behaviour would you see?	What behaviour would you see?	What behaviour would you see?

(Continued)

Choose a situation of your own. Something that is important to you, but that you haven't yet been able to explain from your point of view. Write it below and then practice communicating using the Communication Technique. Don't worry if at first it all feels a bit "clunky." Try saying it out loud to yourself or looking in a mirror. This will help make sure it feels and sounds like you.

Notes

1   Bandura A. (1993). Perceived Self-Efficacy in Cognitive Development and Functioning. *Educational Psychologist*, 28(2), 117–148.
    Bandura A. (2012). On the Functional Properties of Perceived Self-Efficacy Revisited. *Journal of Management*, 38(1), 9–44.
2   Brown B. (2021). *Atlas of the Heart: Mapping Meaningful Connection and the Language of Human Experience*. Vermillion. ISBN-10: 1785043773 ISBN-13: 978-1785043772
3   Dweck CS. (2006). *Mindset: The New Psychology of Success*. Random House.

The sky is falling in   **8**
When our thinking snowballs

Our focus with the skills so far has been to slow things down, to reflect inwards, and to ask questions to help us to build self-awareness. Now we have this understanding, we need skills that can help us take control. Earlier we identified two types of beliefs, *why* beliefs and *what next* beliefs.

What next beliefs can lead to our thinking going into overdrive and snowballing, making a small problem into a big problem, or a big problem into a catastrophic one.

When we catastrophise our attention is future focused as we imagine something alarming: the sky is falling in! That could happen but it probably won't. This vividly imagined event feels very real, as the brain stem and amygdala activate, and adrenalin, the survival hormone, floods our body. At a psychological level we react to our fears.

WoBbLe

Skill

DOI: 10.4324/9781003581994-9

If I miss the train, and I am going to be late picking the kids up on their first day at secondary school, under pressure, panic sets in and my thinking can snowball like this:

- If I am late, they will worry.
- When they worry, they will become anxious.
- The other kids might laugh at them, and they will be embarrassed.
- They won't want to go to school tomorrow.
- They will start missing school.
- They will fall behind and not be able to catch up.
- They will stop going to school and never get an education.

What is catastrophic thinking?

It's thinking that the worst is going to happen, and that negative thinking gets bigger and bigger.

> *It's common because it's part of our survival instinct: our brains are on high alert, looking for danger.*

Catastrophic thinking is a specific distortion of thought that undercuts our psychological resilience. We go into overdrive in a way that can be hard to control, and we need a skill to help us to manage our natural inclination to believe the worst.

None (or at least not all) of the things we are thinking have happened, but they feel like they can in our minds. Our thinking is spiraling, gathering momentum about the worst possible scenario, and we anticipate, without any evidence, extreme and terrible outcomes. This type of thinking is a set of exaggerated negative inaccurate beliefs about things that haven't yet happened.

Imagine this

Carla was home early from work for a change. She looked at the clock; she had fifteen minutes till Ella would be home. Joe was at his maths club and Pete had taken Lily to work for a bring-your-child-to-work day, so she was looking forward to a chance for some quality time with her daughter.

She made a cup of tea and had a quiet moment to shake off her working day and turn her attention to family life. Hearing Ella's key in the front door, she called, "Hi Ells, want a drink?"

Ella came in, dropping her bags. Carla could see immediately that something was bothering her. She hugged her, and Ella rested her head on her mother's shoulder.

"What's up sweetheart?" Carla said.

Ella stepped back and sighed heavily. Her misery was etched in her drooping shoulders and her sad face.

"What happened?"

"It's Chloe's thirteenth birthday next weekend. She's having a party, and everyone has been invited except me!"

Chloe was a year older than Ella, so not a close friend. But Carla could see that Ella felt upset and excluded. "I can understand you feel bad about that."

"It's terrible mum. So embarrassing. I won't be asked to other parties! No one will want to spend any time with me. I'll be a laughingstock."

Carla took a deep inward breath. Her impulse to tell her daughter not to be silly was gripping her, but she used her breathing to control the urge.

Ella was red in the face, and her breathing quickened; she was agitated.

"Everyone will laugh at me, and that will make me angry especially if Mia laughs too, I'll go crazy if she does, and have the biggest row, we'll fall out big time. Then I won't have any friends. I can't go to school; I can't bear it."

Why does this happen?

When our brains are under pressure, the difference between what we imagined and what was real is lost. In those moments when we are worried sick about something that hasn't happened yet, our brains behave as though it actually has happened, and it floods our bodies with fear hormones, primarily adrenalin and cortisol, preparing us for fight or flight. It's the same thing that happened back when we were hunter–gatherers needing to stay safe from sabre-tooth tigers.

> *Catastrophic thinking undercuts our resilience by draining our energy and our ability to think clearly because we are transfixed by the worst possible outcome.*

What can we do about it?

Fortunately, we have a powerful antidote to catastrophising, and it's a skill that we can learn and practise. This will help us to create balance in our minds, to calm our thinking down, so that we are able to think more clearly, and we can decide what to do.

This is an important step, as once catastrophising grips us, it can lead to panic. If our minds continue to snowball, the anxiety builds and, at worst, becomes a panic attack.

Before using this skill, it is useful to use some harnessing emotions techniques to help us press pause, calm down, breathe, and stretch as we take control of the thinking that is disabling our ability to respond helpfully.

The skill to manage catastrophic thinking, WoBble, is a four-step process, in the spirit of an entertaining game to show how we can talk to ourselves in a way that creates balance and puts the situation into perspective.

The best way to learn the skill is to unleash our creativity and imagination, as it's an opportunity to really exaggerate, dramatise, and tell big colorful stories, that will begin in a realistic way, then build and escalate to a grand climax. In other words, to have some fun with the way you can think.

Before we delve into the skill, let's remember that catastrophising is not fun at all. When gripped with negative thoughts that are spiraling, about, for example, a teenager out too late, our fears grip us. Our precious child is out alone, lost, in danger. That's no laughing matter. For anyone who suffers from, or has ever experienced, panic attacks, it's a real and disabling place to be.

But the best way to learn the skill is to be creative and have a little fun, by creating a story. Remember, nothing bad has happened yet.

1. Our first story will create a devastating **worst-case scenario**: that's going to be dark, a tragedy of Shakespearean proportions. We will do this first because that's where our minds go when we catastrophise, so let's exaggerate the way we're thinking about the situation.
2. Then, with our second story we'll turn our mind to creating a thrilling and vivid **best-case scenario**: this will be a fairy tale, a Disney epic of happiness and joy. We will be as extreme as we were in the worst case, but this time to the ridiculously exaggerated best case.
3. Steps 1 and 2 create a balance, as we have forced out the absolute worst, then switched our brain to imagine the fantastically best case. Neither has actually happened, or is likely to, but these steps mean we now have the capacity to think about the **most likely case scenario** based on more balanced thinking.

One of the reasons that balance is created is to do with what happens in the brain when we think of the best case. When we experience positive emotions the neural pathways connect and talk to one another; creative thinking is possible; our intellectual, physical, social, and psychological resources are awake. This balances with the previous step of imagining the worst case which literally shuts the brain connections down, ready for fight or flight.

So force some fun with the best case; it will help you get the best out of the skill.

4. Now we are in position to **list a plan**, the one or two things that will help us deal with the most likely scenario.

Catastrophising is making a mountain out of a molehill or a Himalaya out of a mountain. Whichever you face, it's best to confront it with a balanced brain.

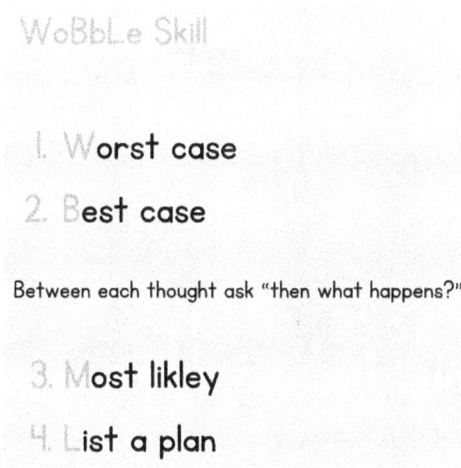

WoBbLe Skill

1. Worst case

2. Best case

Between each thought ask "then what happens?"

3. Most likley

4. List a plan

Back to Ella

"Look Ella, I can see this means a lot to you, but I have an idea, something we could try that might help. It's kind of a game."

Ella shrugged.

"But first you need to take some deep breaths and try and calm down a bit. Let's have that cuppa first and not talk about this while we do. In fact, let's talk about that piece of art you have in your bag. You can tell me how you chose to draw it that way. It looks so detailed."

Twenty minutes later:

"Ok let's try this skill I've been learning in the parent class I've been going to."

"You go to parenting classes?" Ella said.

Carla nodded. "Yep. Me and Dad go. We're learning how to be better parents to you lot, which let me tell you isn't always easy!"

Ella laughed. "You both do great."

Carla smiled. "Shall we give WoBbLe a go? It might help you to think about this in a different way. Right now, you are only seeing the worst case. You are catastrophising. WoBbLe is the name of a skill that will help you balance out your thinking."

"OK," Ella said.

"Ready? There are four steps, so it takes a bit of practice, but it can help when our minds are growing all the worst possible things that could happen. So, let's start with Chloe hasn't invited you to her party and you are embarrassed. What will happen next?"

Ella said, "Everyone will be laughing at me."

"Then what would happen?" Carla asked.

"Even Mia will laugh."

"And then?"

"I'll be angry at her, and we'll argue, and she'll stop talking to me."

"And then?"

"Everyone will take Mia's side, and I won't have any friends, and I won't want to go to school."

"And then?"

"I'll miss class and fall behind."

"And then?"

"I'll have to leave that school! And find a new one."

"What would happen then?"

Ella looked at her mum.

Carla said, "Come on let's keep going, let's make it as bad as it can possibly be."

"I'll start the new school and be in all the bottom sets."

"And then?"

"I'll hate school, I'll have no friends. I'll be a lonely, sad, friendless dropout and I'll never get a job."

"And then?"

"I'd have to live at home forever!" She looked at her mum, and even though it was ridiculous, her eyes showed palpable fear.

Carla took Ella's hand. "That's called catastrophising, when something happens that upsets you, and your thoughts jump to the worst possible things that could happen. Now step two is to switch the thinking. To flip it around and think about the best possible case that would come from Chloe not inviting you to her party. So, let's do that. Chloe hasn't invited you: what is something good that could happen next?"

"Hmm . . ." Ella shrugged.

Carla nudged her. "Come on, use your imagination. What could be good about not being invited to Chloe's party?"

"I know," Ella grinned. "Mia decides not to go too, and we go to the cinema."

"And what would happen next?"

"Mmm . . . it's the opening night and the film actors are there signing autographs."

"Great, you're getting the hang of this. Then what?"

"We were invited to the after-show party, and we got talking to the actors."

"And then?"

"They really like us; they think we're funny and invite us to the film awards to sit at the table with them!"

Carla yelped. "The one that is shown on the TV?"

"Yes! And they win the award, and we're on the telly."

"Wow, then what?"

"Everyone at school wants to know about the night. They think it's amazing and we both get really popular, famous in fact. We both take Drama and later we use our new famous connections, go to drama school, land great parts in the best film and become successful actors!" Ella laughed.

"That's great," Carla said. "Let's just check: are you feeling better?"

"Well yes, but it seems silly. That's never going to happen."

"That's true," Carla said. "And the same is true for the worst case, right?"

Ella shrugged, nodded. "Yeah. Clever."

"See what's happened in your brain? This skill makes you think about the very worst and then the very best case, to create a balance in your mind, and find some perspective about not being invited to the party. Now let's think about the most likely scenario: step three of WoBbLe."

Carla smiled. Inwardly she was deeply relieved as she could see Ella had relaxed. "So, what's the most likely outcome of not being invited to Chloe's' party?"

Ella was thoughtful. "Well, I'm probably not the only person not invited. I'll be sad to miss out. Mia will probably be feeling bad too that I am not going. She knows Chloe because they live on the same street."

Carla said, "There you are, see how the way you are thinking about this is more balanced? You are much calmer. What one or two things can you do to help you deal with the most likely?"

Ella was thoughtful. "Hmm, well, I could arrange to do something else that night?"

"Go to a movie with your Mum?" Carla asked.

"Oh yes, great! and I'll make sure I ask Mia all about the party, all the gossip and what I missed. That will help her feel better about it too."

Carla smiled. "That sounds like a great plan."

"Thanks mum, I do feel so much better." She picked up her bags, kissed Carla, and went to her room to check out what movies were being shown at the cinema.

Something to try

If you are a natural catastrophiser then practising using the skill on your example situations will be helpful. Try using WoBbLe, imagine yourself in the situation and use the four steps to practise.

Some examples for adults to try:

- You are late to an important work meeting
- You take your child's friend to a theme park, and they have gone missing
- You cannot contact your teenager, and they should have been home twenty minutes ago

Activating event:	
1. Worst case	2. Best case
3. Most likely	
4. List your plan	

Summary

Catastrophic thinking is when we believe that the worst is about to happen, and our negative thoughts snowball. It's a specific distortion of thinking that undercuts our energy and ability to think rationally. We have learnt that:

- The antidote to catastrophising is a four-step skill that creates balance in our minds when we are thinking the worst.
- We create two dramatic stories: the worst case, which is where our mind is anyway and so takes things to the extreme; and then the best case, to create balance, to think about the most likely case.
- With the balance of our brain restored, we can plan to deal with the most likely case.

Activities for teenagers

It is vital that you teach WoBbLe in a fun way and not while your child is actually catastrophising about something. The skill needs to be understood and practised with situations that are not their own, so they are familiar with the sequence of steps.

Explain that when we are uncertain about something or somebody, we might assume the worst is going to happen and we can think of this as another set of beliefs: catastrophising Gremlin Beliefs to take control.

Catastrophising Gremlin Beliefs makes us think the worst possible situation is going to happen. It can feel like it really *will* happen.

Catastrophising Gremlin Beliefs are thoughts about things that have not yet happened, but you think will happen in future.

We can think of it as snowballing thoughts in our mind, which grow bigger and bigger and focus on all the worst possible outcomes. Nothing has happened yet, but it feels like it could.

Make a list of things that young people your age might catastrophise about. Not what YOU castrophise about.

-
-
-
-
-

Answer the following questions:

- What is happening inside the body when someone is catastrophising thoughts in their mind?
- How would you describe their thinking?
- What would their voice sound like?
- What is happening to their energy?
- What sorts of things would help someone who is catastrophising?
- What could they do to calm down?

The four steps for controlling catastrophising Gremlin Beliefs before they take over is a crucial skill. Using WoBbLe will help us loosen up and balance our thinking. The order is
important.

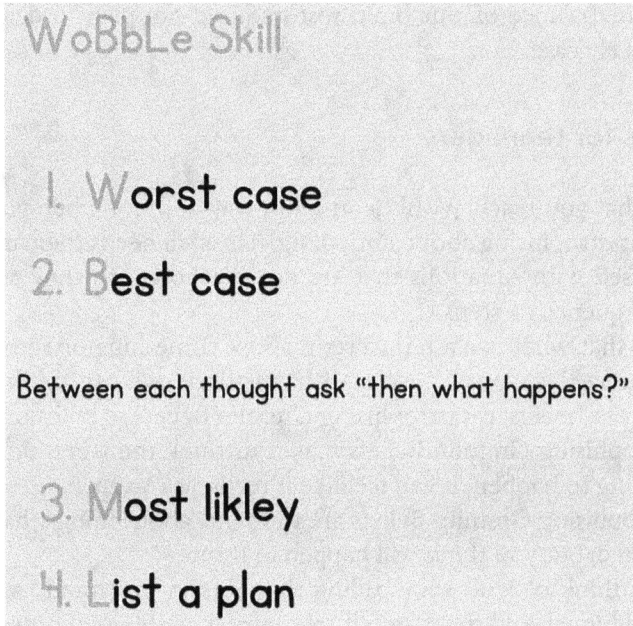

WoBbLe Skill

1. Worst case

2. Best case

Between each thought ask "then what happens?"

3. Most likley

4. List a plan

Practise using WoBbLe.

Activating Event: Calum is about to walk into an exam, and someone says you've been given the wrong revision information.

1. List all the Worst-Case things that could happen next.
    Start with the first negative thing that might pop into his head and then keep asking what would happen next. Each step makes sense, and builds; that's why it feels real. Keep going until the worst possible outcome is reached.
    *   I won't know any answers.
    *   I will fail the exam.
    *   I won't be able to take the subject next year.
    *   I won't get a good job.
    *   I will be unemployed.
    *   On the streets.
    *   I'll become a criminal.
    *   End up in prison.
    Remember none of these things have happened yet. They are all worries about what MIGHT happen, and they are all in Calum's mind.

2. List all the Best-Case things that could happen next.
    Start with the first positive thing and build the list, like with the worst case, until the best possible outcomes have been reached. The best possible outcome needs to be as extreme as the worst case.
    - I know all the answers.
    - I get the highest mark in the country.
    - Reporters come to the school to interview me.
    - The story goes viral.
    - A top firm recruits me.
    - A film company makes a film about me.
    - I inspire a generation.

    Remember none of these things have happened yet. Thinking about all the best possible outcomes balances the mind, and calms us down, sometimes by making us laugh.

3. List the Most Likely.
    - There are some questions I don't know.
    - I won't do as well in the exam as I would have liked.
    - I do answer some questions.

4. Plan how to deal with the most likely.
    - Talk to my teacher about the revision information to see if lots of other people are in the same boat.
    - Talk to my teacher about what happens if I fail; can I re-sit, what will the real impact be?
    - Focus on the exams yet to come and how I can plan better.
    - Focus on my achievements: I think I have done really well in other exams.

    Now try using WoBbLe with the examples provided. Remember to use the order.

    Practice Examples:
    - Denver has arranged a virtual meetup that everyone has been talking about. Seconds before it starts, a friend messages to say a friend Denver meant to invite, but didn't, is really angry with her.
    - Liam posted a picture by mistake and it already has fifty likes.
    - Choose a situation of your choice that someone your age might worry about and use.

Calming down

When the mind begins to snowball thoughts, the energy rises, and the situation heats up. Knowing how to calm down can be a useful first step.

Mental stillness

Use your finger to trace your way around the maze. As you do breathe gently and relax into finding your way through.

When you know the route, colour it in.

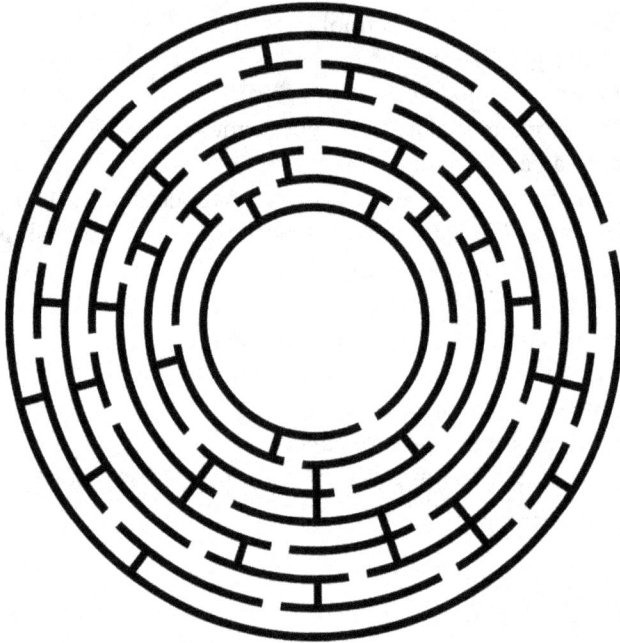

Pursed lip breathing

Sit upright in your chair, get comfortable, but feel present in your seat. Close your eyes or lower your gaze and find a spot to focus on.

Keeping your mouth closed, inhale slowly through your nose for 2 counts, 1, 2.

Pucker or purse your lips as though you are going to whistle, but don't whistle.

Exhale slowly by blowing air through your pursed lips for a count of four, 1, 2, 3, 4.

Now try that again, inhale slowly through your nose, 1, 2.

Pucker or purse your lips as though you are going to whistle, but don't whistle.

Exhale slowly by blowing air through your pursed lips for a count of 1, 2, 3, 4.

Repeat for a few rounds.

Equal breathing

Sit upright in your chair, get comfortable, but feel present in your seat. Close your eyes or lower your gaze and find a spot to focus on.

Breathe slowly and deeply in through your nose and out through your mouth.

Count during each inhale and exhale to make sure they are even in length.

Starting with a count of three, then four, then five.

Take a slight pause after each inhale and exhale.

Choose a word or short phrase to repeat during each inhale and exhale. *I am proud of me* or something similar and positive.

One step beyond

9

The power of moving on

What gets in the way of changing how we think? The simple answer is: we do. We tend to notice, and have a bias towards, things that confirm that we're right. Why? Because it keeps us safe, within our familiar sphere of comfort. We don't want to be wrong, because we fear looking bad or feeling vulnerable.

Being able to make sense of information quickly can be beneficial. Forming new explanations takes energy and effort, so we have adapted over time to take the path of least resistance. There are good evolutionary reasons to think fast: imagine our hunter–gatherer ancestors, faced with a charging and intimidating animal: quick thinking means they were able to act rapidly and survive.

Confirmation bias[1]

We are safer in groups, having a greater chance of survival than being alone. We hold onto what we believe to be true, and we seek out others who

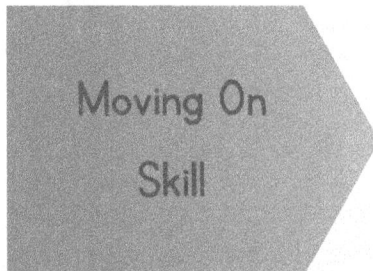

Moving On

Skill

DOI: 10.4324/9781003581994-10

agree. Being wrong makes us more vulnerable, and perhaps alone. On the upside our confirmation bias keeps us safe. However, less positively, it can prevent us from changing how we think, and this is a problem when the way we're thinking is leading to unhelpful consequences.

If we want to feel better, and behave in more productive ways, we need to challenge how we are thinking. But the evidence that tells us we are wrong can be hard to see: our confirmation bias again. To really change what we believe to be true about something, we must work hard to look for evidence that passes our own gut test. We can't kid ourselves into a new way of thinking. We must reflect deeply so that we can think and feel differently in an authentic way. We all know what it's like to be presented with a viewpoint that we disagree with: we dismiss it, and justify to ourselves and others why it simply isn't true.

Some ways to avoid the confirmation bias include:

- Imagine the complete opposite of what you think is true and see how it changes the outcome.
- Ask someone you respect or trust to help you find a reason you might be wrong.
- Think of the situation from a different perspective; stand in the shoes of others.
- Write it down in a story and find different endings with different outcomes.

Imagine this

When Ella and Pete returned from the shop to buy the eggs for cookery, Carla could see that they'd had words of some kind. They both looked moody, and Ella went straight to her room.

"Has something happened?" she asked.

"It's unbelievable," Pete said. "You'll never guess what she told me."

"OK I won't try. What was it?"

"She said I'm nicer to Lily than I am to her. She said Lily's my favourite. That I treat her differently. Totally incredible eh!"

Carla stayed quiet.

Pete, bewildered, said, "I don't, do I?"

"Actually, Pete you do."

"When?"

"Well, she's the only child that you've read to every night at bedtime," Carla said.

Pete said, "I don't understand it, that's just me being a good dad! Surely?"

Carla said, "Look Pete, Lily is the baby of the family and the apple of your eye. It's plain to see, everybody knows."

"But I stopped reading to Ella because she didn't want me to read to her!" Pete turned away from Carla and shouted, "I can't get anything right, I'm a good dad and all I get is criticism." He walked out of the room, took his coat and keys, and left the house.

Pete drove off, thinking to himself, "I am a good dad. Most dads I know don't read to their kids every night, go out at all hours to buy cookery ingredients, work, run the football team, they could do a lot worse than me."

He felt more and more annoyed. Then a light flashed: he'd been caught by a camera doing 36 in a 30mph street.

Pause for reflection

Consider:
- Is the way Pete is feeling or behaving helping or hindering him?
- Are his beliefs about being a good dad helping him to decide what to do next?
- Is he dealing with this situation well?

Pete was relying on some habits of thinking here that he needed to challenge, because they were not helping him.

What's the goal?

First Pete needed to think about what he wanted the outcome to be. A closer relationship with Ella? Being a more all-round better dad? To be at home with his family, not out getting speeding tickets?

Changing the way we think about something, particularly something we care about, is hard. When we challenge our beliefs, we aren't just trying to feel better or pretend that everything is fine as it is. Sometimes it may be worse, at least to begin with. In Pete's case, accepting that he might be part of the reason that he stopped reading to Ella was not easy.

We can only respond helpfully to a situation once we have a realistic view of it. Resilience comes from being as accurate as possible, not thinking that it is worse than it is on the one hand or pretending that it is better on the other. Our habits of thought mean we miss information, so we need to seek out what we are missing to gain a better understanding. Confirmation bias means new evidence is hard to see and accept, but once we can think differently, we can make more sense of what's happened. When we arrive at this point, we can truly solve problems and use our resilience to move forward in a helpful way.

The Moving On skill builds on the ABC and Reframing skills by adding a step that helps us to challenge and change what we believe to be true.

Something to try

ABC the situation – go back to Chapter 4 to review.

Look at your Beliefs – and code them. Determine whether they are:

- Me
- Them
- Always

Use helpful questions

- Me: how did others contribute? What external factor was at play here?
- Them: how did I contribute? What is in my control?
- Always: how long will this last? What is changeable?

Now get tough with your thinking. Don't stay with your original beliefs, or a version of them. Be prepared to really challenge how you think. It's like being a good detective with your own thoughts. This part can sometimes be easier if you involve someone else. Be clear what you need from them.

"Hey Voula, I have this situation, that I would like to understand better, but I keep getting stuck in my own head. Here is where I am so far."

Share the ABC and the habits, and be clear what you need from them. For example, can you help me:

- See what I might be missing?
- See it from their perspective?
- Understand how you would deal with this?
- Tell me what you think I could do?

When asking a friend to help, use a timer, and explain: "Look I only want to talk about this for ten or fifteen minutes, and then let's talk about something else."

Be clear with your friend about their role. If we don't set a time limit, we risk talking for too long, and just end up where we started, instead of somewhere helpful.

Remember the goal and be prepared to feel uncomfortable when noticing what might have been missed. When we recognise we were wrong, it can be hard, because of the implications: we may have to do something different, take ourselves out of our comfort zone, and that can be a big step.

Imagine this

Pete ABCs the situation.

Activating event: Ella said to Pete that her younger sister Lily was his favourite. His wife Carla agreed stating that Lily was the only child he read to.

Pete's beliefs in the moment:	What's the habit?
1. I'm a good dad	1. Always
2. I can't get anything right	2. Me and always
3. All I get is criticism	3. Them and always
4. I only stopped reading to Ella because she didnt want me to	4. Them

Consequences at the time: Pete walks out of the room, ignores Ella and Lily on his way out. He feels annoyed. Loses concentration driving and gets flashed by a speed camera for driving over the limit.

He uses helpful questions to help him reframe his habits a little.
I'm a good dad.

- It is true, I am a good dad, but Ella doesn't think so right now, and I have stopped reading to her.

I can't be right all the time.

- I'm right a lot of the time
- I took Ella to the grocery shop at short notice
- I run Joe's football team
- I read to Lily every night

All I get is criticism.

- That's not true; the kids and Carla say some pretty lovely things to me and often show me they are grateful for the things I do.
- I only stopped reading to Ella because she didn't want me to.
- I actually don't know why I stopped reading; it just sort of happened.
- I thought she was getting too old for it.

Pete felt a bit trapped. He could see that he had reacted unhelpfully, but he needed some support, so he sat down with Carla. He explained his ABC and reframing work and asked her to help him to see what he was missing. They agreed to time themselves for fifteen minutes and then to stop talking about it. Carla also promised not to try and tell Pete what to do. That was up to him.

"Let's go through your reframing and maybe push a bit more on how you are thinking about this. First, out of everything you have written what is the most upsetting part?"

"That Ella thinks Lily is my favourite," Pete replied.

Carla pushed: "You thought that Ella was getting too old to read to her, what led you to that?"

"I'm not really sure," Pete said, "I suppose it's more to do with the time I have in the evening, you know how stretched it all gets, and Lily is still so young. I just stopped prioritising it. Ella has homework to do."

"So, the reason you stopped reading to Ella is to do with time, not her getting too old. What do you do with Ella, just with her on her own?" Carla asked.

"I don't do anything with Joe alone either!" Pete snapped. His stomach was churning, and he felt suddenly guilty.

"You do football with Joe. I know you have the other kids there but it's something you share."

"Yes I can see that, Ella feels left out, but I love her just as much as the other two."

"Of course you do Pete, you do loads for her, and all of them. You're a great dad, and they are lucky to have you, as am I, most of the time. That's the fifteen minutes, so I'm going to leave it with you. Unless you want me to help you think about what to do."

"No, I can do this," Pete said.

The next day Pete asked Ella if she wanted to go for a drive with him. He thought it would help him to say what he wanted to Ella without it feeling too intense.

"I'm glad you agreed to come for a drive Ella because I wanted to talk to you about you saying that Lily was my favourite."

Ella glanced at her dad. "Sorry," she said.

"It's ok Ella, it actually made me think about what we do together, and I realised we don't. I miss the chats we used to have. I wondered if you miss them too?"

"I can't remember the last time we were on our own together, can you?" Ella asked.

"No, and I want to change that. I was thinking that the evenings were so busy, for both of us, that we didn't have time to do stuff together, and to be honest, I thought you were too old to have a story from your dad!"

"Well yeah, I am a bit old for Winnie the Pooh."

Pete asked, "Anything you'd like us to do? Maybe we could have something we could do once a week together?"

"I've started playing darts at school. I'm getting quite good."

"Darts! I didn't think you were going to say that! There's actually a darts board in the loft, from when I was a kid. I'll find it."

"Amazing dad, I'd love that. Can you drop me at Mia's now please?"

"Sure." Pete leaned over and hugged her tight.

Summary

The skill of mental resilience becomes a superpower when we are able to challenge and change how we think. Then we can really move on from an old thinking pattern because we can see the benefit of doing so. We have learnt that:

- The moving on skill builds on the ABC and reframing skills by adding a step that helps us to challenge and change what we believe to be true.
- It is brave to recognise that the way we are thinking is creating a problem, for ourselves, and perhaps those around us, but doing so means we can truly move forward.
- We need to look hard for evidence that we have missed. Asking a friend might help us overcome the confirmation bias.
- Stay focused on the goal: what it is that you want to achieve.

Activities for teenagers

The purpose is to build the capacity for flexible and realistic thinking. The activities introduce the skill of looking for different ways of seeing a situation, to change and challenge one's perspective as the route to a better outcome. The aim is to teach our teenagers the difference between helpful and unhelpful thoughts, and learn that thinking flexibly and realistically is a mental strength.

Being a detective

Which detective would you rather hire to help you solve a crime? Write down what it is about their approach that you think is better.

Detective one

Asks lots of questions. Considers all the facts. Looks for evidence. Discusses ideas with a trusted colleague.

Detective two

Arrests the first person that comes to mind.

Now be detective one and help these characters see what they might be missing and what the alternative way to think about the situation could be.

Activating Event	What are they missing?	What would be a credible alternative way to think about this?
Esra is in trouble for not completing her homework. She thinks "Homework is a complete waste of time, I don't learn anything from it and the teacher is picking on me."		
Kylo's parents have both started working at home. So much so they haven't really had much time to help him with his schoolwork and he is struggling. He thinks "My work isn't important. They will get angry if I interrupt them. They don't care about me."		
Keily is sixteen and bored of being stuck at home as she has been grounded and not able to see her friends. She sneaks out to meet her friends at the park. She thinks "What harm am I doing? They won't even realise I have gone."		

Note

1   Nickerson RS. (1998). Confirmation Bias: A Ubiquitous Phenomenon in Many Guises. *Review of General Psychology*, 2(2), 175–220. https://doi.org/10.1037/1089-2680.2.2.175
See suggested reading in Chapter 13.

Making it real

Resilience in action

10

The benefits of personal resilience are most powerful when we become practised enough to use the skills in the moment. We will know and trust them enough, so as things happen, we can deal effectively with the situation right then and there.

We talked earlier about not sweating the small stuff, but equally not ignoring it either. The situations we face every day create challenges to a greater or lesser degree, depending on all sorts of factors: the amount we are juggling; the severity of the situation; the time at which matters arise. Some events are clearly stressful whilst others we ignore, but they are having an impact on mind and body. The saying "the straw that broke the camel's back" is founded in science and called allostatic load. That's a cumulative measure of the impact of our life events. When they build up, they affect both physical and psychological well-being, so learning skills that can mitigate the accumulation, to not let things fester, and to pay attention to the tiny niggles is a way to pay it forward that really matters.

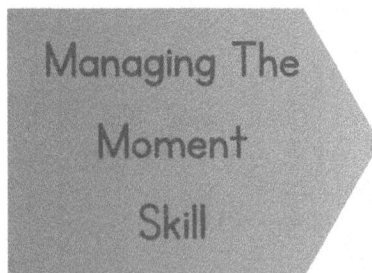

Managing The

Moment

Skill

DOI: 10.4324/9781003581994-11

Practise, fast and slow

Reoccurring, tricky, more complex situations require time, for us to practice using the skills in a slow way, on our own, sat at a table with a page of this book open, working it through. Going back to what happened and taking our time to understand is necessary to reach the outcome that will be most useful, to prevent the allostatic load, and to develop self-efficacy in the face of the prevailing context. As we practise the skills more and more, it gradually starts to play into the way we respond.

Over time we become skilled at managing effectively in the moment.

Where learning takes place

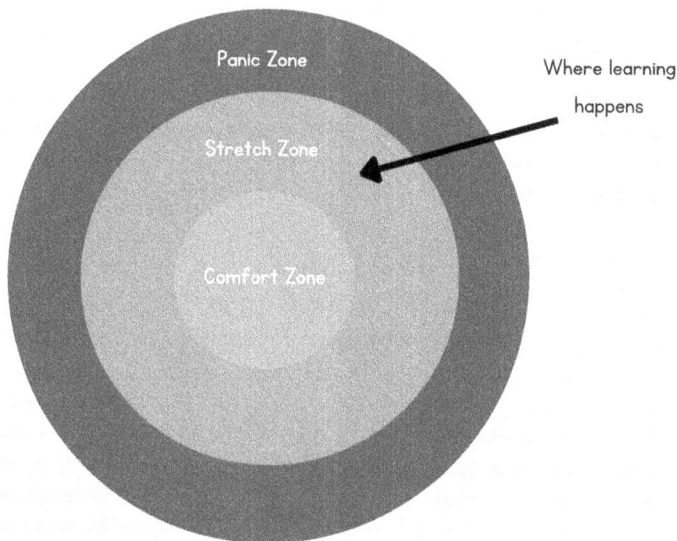

- Our comfort zone is where we can relax because we know what we're doing, and we are at ease.
- The stretch zone, the space between our comfort zone and our panic zone, is where we learn new things.
- The panic zone is where everything feels like too much, we feel overstretched, and we feel alarmed. This not a nice place to be. When we find ourselves here, we must act and use the harnessing emotions strategies to control our instinctual impulse to calm down and reset.

The reason for explaining the importance of where learning happens is to ensure we stretch in the right way for ourselves and our teenagers.

Something to try

Make a note of the time on your clock; start a stopwatch. Now, hold one of your arms out in front of you at roughly ninety degrees. As you do pay full attention to what is going on. Is your hand fizzing, your elbow creaking, your arm warm? Put all your attention into your arm, notice the point at which it starts to feel uncomfortable; is it seconds or minutes? At a certain point, your arm will start to feel heavy, to pull at your shoulder or neck, it will start to feel uncomfortable. When it does relax it down; give it a gentle rub.

Notice your thoughts: what are you thinking right now, how are you feeling? What else is happening in your body?

The activity is a simple way to introduce the concept of being out of the comfort zone. Your arm is not used to being held out in front of you, and so quickly both your mind and your body start to tell you. Now if you were to repeat the process each day the length of time you could hold your arm out would increase. Your mind and body would become more familiar with the action; it will be learning and storing memory and building muscle.

This same concept can be applied to using the skills of psychological fitness. Learning how to use them will feel strange at first, even clunky and uncomfortable, like holding your arm out when it is not used to it. But the payoff is that you are mentally stronger, you are better able to cope with the challenges you face, and you feel effective and confident in your capacity.

Using process praise to encourage growth

We don't want to feel uncomfortable and the idea of pushing our children out of their comfort zone may feel like an alien concept particularly when the presence of danger is never far from our screens. But it's where learning happens, and so if we never experience being uncomfortable, we can't grow or be at our best.

We like to think of the stretch zone as the brave push we need, because we know it will be worth it. No pain, no gain, right? Using process praise to reward the willingness to push out and learn something is a powerful approach. Remember we all respond to praise.

- I could see you struggling, so you changed your approach, well done; can you help me with something I have been struggling with?

- I am so proud that you didn't give up, even though I know you had to work super hard.
- It was so cool seeing you take a breather before trying again.
- Walking away was a smart move because they were not going to budge.
- I know it's hard when you say something you regret, but the way you explained what happened and the reasons you got it wrong when you apologised, that was very brave.

> *Nudge your children along, bit by bit, to model the behaviour you want to encourage in them.*

Push them enough, but not so hard that they give up and stop. This is more likely to mean they see the value in the skills, and it will keep lines of communication open, as they trust your advice and see for themselves that you are a good source of support.

Shortcut skills that help us to get through

The potential gains for spending time learning the skills have been clearly laid out, yet sometimes, we need a quick way of responding that is good enough to get through the next hour or day. It can be as simple as:

- Batting away a negative thought by replacing it with a more optimistic one
- Explaining to yourself why something is not completely true
- Jumping to the best possible outcome to create some quick mental balance

These ideas are not something to rely on all the time because they won't create the lasting change that we have discussed so far, but they can be enough to get you through. To give you that burst of self-confidence you need in the moment.

With this in mind, let's explore how the skills can be applied in the moment, by showing how our family did it.

Imagine this

Carla and Joe

Carla was worried about Joe, because he had been quieter than usual recently and she didn't really know what was going on with him. She hadn't spent much time with him, so she felt a bit disconnected.

It was the weekend, and Joe had said he was feeling a bit unwell and didn't want to go to football. He asked Carla to tell Pete.

Carla didn't want to pry; he was probably fine and best left on his own. But she did a mini-ABC in her head and the truth was that she was concerned that he was quiet. This more realistic version of what was going on gave her some options.

She asked herself: was it better to tell Joe that she had noticed he was quiet? or suggest he tell Pete himself that he didn't want to go to football to force his hand a bit? She decided to check in on him.

Joe was in the kitchen. Carla said, "Oh love do me a favour and make me a coffee."

Joe sighed and filled the kettle.

"I've noticed you've been quieter than usual recently and I wanted to check in with my favourite son. How's things?" Carla said.

"Your only son," Joe said. "I'm alright – just loads of work."

Carla said, "Anything I can help with?"

"Not unless you can help me understand trigonometry! I have an exam next week."

"Maths is not my strong point, but maybe I could understand some of it. Sometimes two heads can be better than one. Have you spoken to the maths teacher?" Carla said.

"Yes, but I don't understand what she is saying. I ask a question then I don't get the answer. If you could look at it with me, and maybe help me with the right question to ask?"

Joe brought the coffee over. Carla smiled at him. "Thanks Joe. Go and grab your books."

Joe and Carla spent the next hour together. Although Carla couldn't give him any answers, she did suggest asking for extra time with his teacher, and Joe thought that was a good idea.

By using ABC, and reframing in the moment, Carla responded in a way that meant she and Joe had time together. The problem wasn't solved but they had connected, kept lines of communication open, and Carla had shown Joe that she was willing to help.

Ella

Ella and Mia had been friends since primary school. Recently they had spent less time together, because of their different timetables, they went to different clubs, and Mia walked to school with the girls in her road.

They had arranged to meet up after school and Ella was looking forward to it. That morning, she posted an old school picture of her and Mia on Instagram. While she waited for her to arrive, she looked at her Insta and saw that Chloe, a friend who lived in the same street as Mia, had added a hysterical face with a comment: @mia is that really you, look at your hair?! and a frizz ball emoji. Ella could see that Mia had seen the post, but she had not commented, and now she was late. Ella started to think the worst: I shouldn't have posted that stupid picture. I've embarrassed her, she is so mad at me and doesn't want to be friends anymore. Her hands felt clammy; her heart was racing; her thoughts were beginning to snowball: I'm catastrophising. I need to calm down.

She took a moment, drew around her hand, taking slow deep breaths as she traced around her fingers, pausing at the top of each and holding her breath before breathing out, as she traced down the other side. By the time she finished she felt calmer. She tried the simple breathing techniques that she and her and mum had been doing together.

Ok, she said to herself, I'll do a shortcut WoBbLe: what's the very worst that could happen here? Mia hates me and never wants to be friends again.

Ok, now let me flip this, what's the very best that could happen? Mia thinks the photo is the best and that Chloe is nasty and stops being friends with her.

Ella grinned to herself because this thought made her smile, and she immediately felt more balanced in her head. Now what's the most likely? Mia isn't keen on the photo but hasn't had time to think whether she wants to respond. So, I'll wait a few more minutes here and then give Mia a call to see where she is and ask if everything is ok.

Just at that moment Ella saw Mia running towards her. "Sorry," she called. "We were all kept back after school because I was caught with my phone in class." Mia was panting as she got to Ella. "I was showing Bryony that picture you posted, and she was laughing so much at my ridiculous hair, what were we like!"

"You didn't mind?" Ella asked. "I probably should have checked with you first."

"I think it's great," said Mia, "I can't believe how much we have changed."

"Did you see the comment Chloe added?" asked Ella.

"Yeah, I'd like to see what her hair was like back in the day!" Mia laughed.

Mia hooked into Ella's arm as they started walking. "Right where are we going? We have so much to catch up on. I've missed you."

"Me too," Ella replied, "let's go into town for a coffee."

By using a breathing technique Ella calmed herself down. Then, using the shorthand version of WoBbLe allowed Ella to keep things in perspective about how Mia would react, rather than panic about it. Instead, she calmed herself down, balanced her mind, and learned firsthand that thinking the worst can be a waste of energy.

Joe

As we found out earlier, Joe was finding maths difficult. He was in a double maths lesson, to prepare for a mock exam at the end of the month. He really needed to understand trigonometry. The lesson was underway, and Mrs Evans had set them a task and asked if anyone had any questions.

Joe was thinking, "I am going to look dumb in front of everyone." Then he realised that this was fixed thinking, so he reframed it to, "Other people may be finding it hard as well, so me asking a question might help them too."

His next thought was: "She thinks I'm annoying, because I just don't understand what she is saying." Then he recognised that this was an unhelpful thought that didn't help him. "That's not completely true," he thought, "because she has offered me help before, and she did just ask if anyone has questions."

Joe raised his hand, and the teacher said, "Yes Joe?"

He said, "I know you have explained this before, but I just can't get my head around it. Is there a different way of explaining it, what am I missing?"

Mrs Evans said, "Thanks Joe, yes, it is tricky, let me try a different way." She illustrated it with a picture of a triangle and used a scenario to explain the formula. "Give this a go and see if it helps you find the ratio."

Joe found the image very helpful and drew it in his notebook.

By using the resilience skills in real time, Joe practised being outside his comfort zone. He quickly batted away his unhelpful and inaccurate beliefs, and, most importantly, he asked the question.

Something to try

When you recognise your beliefs getting in the way, like they did for Carla, Ella, and Joe, using a shorthand version of the skills can be useful, in the moment. It's not always possible to sit down and go through the longhand process, and so the shortcuts are enough to get you through.

When you recognise a belief that is in your way, you can help yourself by either:

- Coming up with some evidence to discount or oppose the way you are thinking about it: That's not true because . . .
- Reframe the way you are thinking about something by choosing an alternative, more optimistic way of seeing the situation: Another way of seeing this could be . . .
- Doing a quick worst case, best case in your mind: The most likely outcome is. . . . And I can . . .

If later when you reflect and notice that it's a recurring situation, or something you are still thinking about, perhaps late at night, or a week later, that's when you know you need the longhand version of the skill to slow things down and spend time thinking through and working out what is going on here.

Nurturing the optimistic muscle

Making the skills real for yourself will be enhanced if you nurture your optimistic muscle and use positive emotions to build your skills into everyday life. Remember, optimism is a choice, it's a way of thinking. It is not ignoring the difficulties that are around but it's an intentional decision to pay attention to the good around you, or the parts where you have some control.

Expressing gratitude more often is fabulous for personal well-being, and for nurturing the optimistic muscle. When we look around more intently for the good bits, what is going well, what I can be grateful for, the wonder in the world around me, these open our mind to optimism. When we express our gratitude to others, it not only helps them feel good, but it also has personal benefits. Like with everything, the more we do it, the more comfortable it becomes.

Here are a few ideas for developing optimism:

- At the end of each day, think of three good things that have happened. They can be big or small, maybe something you have done or that you've noticed in others. Something that made you smile, helped you, or the way you helped others, or things you feel proud of. Start a journal of the things you can be grateful for; writing them down will make them stay with you for longer.
- Create a good things box that you fill up over the year, a place to collect the wonderful things that happen for you and your family. Then on a special day when you are all together, Christmas or another family tradition, bring them out and share them. Thank them for the joy they brought you. Take each one in turn, as if you are gifting a reminder of the moment back to the person.
- Share good things with others. When we articulate and say them out loud, we are creating a stronger, richer moment for ourselves that will stay with us, and the people we are telling, for longer. We are social beings, and we thrive when we connect in a meaningful way with others.

- Use positive emotion, even in the difficult moments. Use laughter to help to cope and deal with difficult situations. Positive emotion is not a nice to-do, it's a strategy (remind yourself in Chapter 3).
- Spend time thinking about what makes you laugh: save that funny video, belly dance like no one is watching, use the comedic side of your personality, however hidden, to experience positive emotion.

Reasons not to teach shortcuts to teenagers

In the 21st century, fast is good. Everything is available at the touch of a button; we order something today and expect to receive it tomorrow. We want quick solutions, and a superficial one-liner. A thirty-second video often receives more attention than something of deeper meaning. When it comes to personal growth however, then quick is not necessarily the best in the long term. The gratification of spending time learning the skills of psychological fitness does not come overnight, although, as adults, sometimes we hit a lightbulb moment that changes our path.

When it comes to teaching teenagers the skills then longhand is always going to offer more value. For this reason, we discourage you from explicitly teaching the shortcut skills. Children are smart; if you support them in the right way, and introduce the skills in a thoughtful way that feels authentic, then they will devise their own shortcuts. Look out for these; notice and praise them when you see them. Use explicit process praise when you do: "I notice you slowed the way you were thinking down and listened out for unhelpful gremlins; that was so smart."

Summary

Psychological fitness grows and expands over time. It is not a quick fix; it takes time to develop and understand what is going to work best for you, and when. We have learnt that:

- By investing in learning the skills and teaching them to children we are laying down helpful pathways for personal growth.
- Once we know the skills well, we can also create shortcut versions that we can use in the moments when we need to be good enough.
- The optimistic muscle needs exercising and there are many ways to strengthen it.
- We encourage you to teach your teenagers the longhand version of the skills. When they are ready, they will make their own versions of them.

You are one of a kind   **11**

Using unique strengths to thrive

We all have unique qualities and strengths that define us, that are valuable personally and to others. If we identify them, we can use them to be at our best, and to understand when they are getting in the way and holding us back.

When it comes to personal strengths, there are a couple of challenges. The first is that we are not very good at talking about what we're great at. We can hold beliefs like: it's showing off, being a big head, not very cool. Sometimes our strengths get in our way, and we need to dial them down to get the most out of a situation. Secondly, there are times when we are specifically asked about our strengths, in a job interview for example, and it can be difficult to find the words to articulate our unique qualities.

The good news is that twenty-five years ago social scientists set about helping us with both of these. An extensive research project that identified twenty-four character strengths, or positive virtues, was developed, along with a questionnaire that would allow people to identify their own top

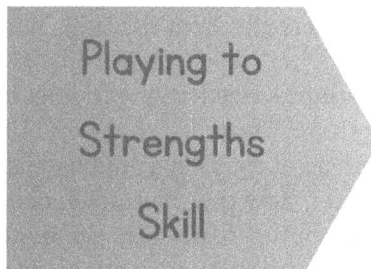

Playing to Strengths Skill

DOI: 10.4324/9781003581994-12

character strengths. The capacity to play to our strengths is both an in-depth self-awareness tool *and* a superpower.

Knowing our unique strengths isn't just interesting information – although how wonderful it would be if we could spend time thinking about what makes us uniquely individual – but, when skilfully used, they can have a significant effect on our self-awareness, our self-confidence, our self-belief, and our self-acceptance, with all the knock-on effects of those advantages.

Knowing and using our strengths can help to:

- Buffer against, manage, and overcome problems
- Improve relationships
- Enhance health and overall well-being

As we have seen, we all have a pull to the negative, as we explored in Chapter 2, to remember criticism, to prioritise danger over joy, to be drawn to the shocking headlines, and to focus on weaknesses and deficits. This instinctive drive has played out in everyday life: strengths are something to reveal only in certain situations. We are generalising of course, as many of us will be confident in knowing what we are good at, but many of us don't, so the aim here is to refocus our thinking, to understand the value in noticing the positive, and to bring out the very best in ourselves.

Lucy's early career

In my early career I worked with young people who were in the care system, having been let down by the adults around them in some way or another. My work was to support them to transition from residential care to independent living, a massive step, not least because they were doing it largely on their own. Once teenagers reached eighteen years of age they were viewed as adults and therefore able to go out into the world and fend for themselves. Much work went into planning how to make the transition better for these young people, and I used to work with them for around eight weeks to teach them the skills we have been sharing in this book.

One of the first questions I asked, to get to know them and build trust, was about their strengths. Without fail they would look at me as if I had asked them if they were an alien. They could have spoken at length about their flaws and weaknesses, how they had failed, been in trouble at school, with police, been kicked out of foster care. Honestly, they could talk for hours. Yet one simple question about their strengths stumped them.

How sad, I thought; these children had experienced troubled, yet rich and colourful lives, but they had survived, they still had the gumption to keep going, to fight. They should be singing about their experiences from the rooftops, helping us learn about life through their lenses, not hiding away, too cautious to show themselves and their experiences. Nothing brought me more joy than receiving their character strengths survey results, and sitting down with them to reflect on how and when they were in play, and how they would be helpful moving forward.

Things I love about people

Human beings are creative, brave, modest, loyal, kind, funny, spiritual, inventive, curious, cautious, honest, forgiving. We all have these qualities to some extent, and they are all things we like, value, and respect.

The character strength survey looked deeply into understanding human traits, to ensure these qualities could be:

- recognised regardless of geography,
- found everywhere, and in shining examples,
- not linked to gender or culture.

> *In other words, external differences didn't matter, these qualities could make sense to people everywhere.*

The twenty-four character strengths were all described in detail to show what it means when they are part of a person's character.

For example, Judgement is described as:

- Thinking things through and examining them from all sides.
- Not jumping to conclusions.
- Being able to change one's mind in the light of evidence.
- Weighing all evidence fairly.

Alongside, a brilliant tool was developed: a strengths survey, a set of statements that individuals would decide if that was a lot like them, some-what like them, or not like them.

The aim of the validated tool was to help individuals identify their strengths as a pathway to understanding themselves.

The twenty-four character strengths are grouped under six main headings: Wisdom, Courage, Humanity, Justice, Temperance, and Transcendence,

We have all these strengths to a lesser or greater degree. Our top five strengths, or the combination of them, are unique to us.

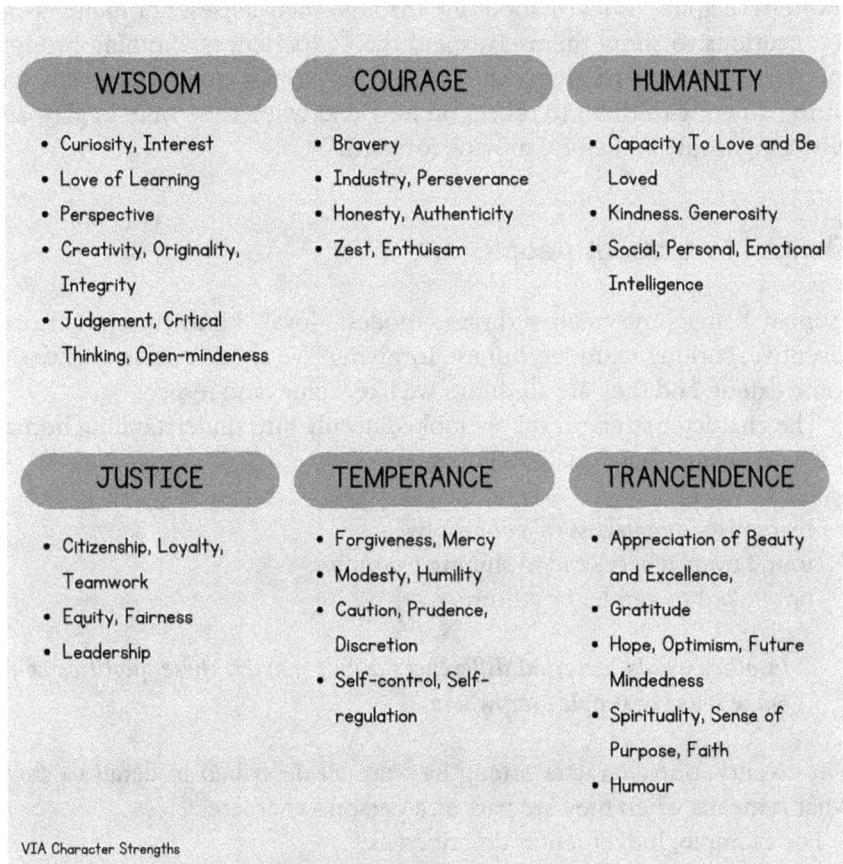

WISDOM
- Curiosity, Interest
- Love of Learning
- Perspective
- Creativity, Originality, Integrity
- Judgement, Critical Thinking, Open-mindeness

COURAGE
- Bravery
- Industry, Perseverance
- Honesty, Authenticity
- Zest, Enthuisam

HUMANITY
- Capacity To Love and Be Loved
- Kindness. Generosity
- Social, Personal, Emotional Intelligence

JUSTICE
- Citizenship, Loyalty, Teamwork
- Equity, Fairness
- Leadership

TEMPERANCE
- Forgiveness, Mercy
- Modesty, Humility
- Caution, Prudence, Discretion
- Self-control, Self-regulation

TRANCENDENCE
- Appreciation of Beauty and Excellence,
- Gratitude
- Hope, Optimism, Future Mindedness
- Spirituality, Sense of Purpose, Faith
- Humour

VIA Character Strengths

Figure 11.2

The number of potential character strengths profiles is exponentially greater than the number of people living on our planet.

This is regardless of diversity, neuro or otherwise, physical ability or disability, the circumstances in which we live, our gender, class, ethnicity.

These strengths are personal and unique, and they also connect us because they offer a shared way to articulate and rejoice in our strengths and capacities.

You may look at the list and be drawn to some as being better to have than others, but there is no hierarchy. All twenty-four are of equal value, though we may find ourselves judging some as better or worse than others.

Something to think about

In 2014, 4,000 soldiers took the strengths survey, a piece of work commissioned by senior officials to find out the top qualities. At the same time all soldiers were taught the skills in this book as part of their introductory training.

Something to think about

Look at the list of twenty-four strengths in Figure 11.2: which do you think came out as the most common top strength across the four-thousand soldiers?

The answer was: the capacity to **love and be loved**.

Surprisingly, this was not a disappointment to their seniors, who were delighted that their soldiers had the strength and capacity to both give and receive love. Think about this. There is a vulnerability in the ability to be close enough to another person to both give and receive love; it's being able to do both that is the strength. Then think about this in the context of those who have chosen a career to literally put their lives on the line to protect others. To die for their country. Imagine being on the front line next to a fellow soldier who has the capacity, the strength within them, to love and be loved.

What we are good at and what we value tend to align. That's possibly why we are drawn to some of the qualities in the list more than others, because personal strengths are linked to the things we value.

Our strengths can both help and hinder, and so it takes self-awareness to manage them effectively. For example, there are times when being honest is going to be super helpful because it helps to build trust with others, allows for open communication, and creates respect. Other times honesty may need to be dialed down. Telling your friend you don't like her outfit a few minutes before you go out is probably not going to be welcomed. The same is true for all the strengths. Judgement is a helpful quality when there is time to weigh everything up, but less helpful if the building is on fire and a fast response is needed.

Using our strengths can be used to achieve positive personal outcomes.

Imagine this

Carla knew she was a good mum, wife, and colleague: not perfect by any stretch of the imagination, but she worked hard to get things right as much as possible. As the kids were growing older, she had forgotten herself a bit, as she focused on supporting everyone else. She found it hard to remember what she loved about herself before she had all the responsibility of looking after others.

At a recent work appraisal, she was asked if there was anything she wanted to discuss about herself. She felt that her efforts had not really been captured but she couldn't articulate what was missing, so she had just said she was happy.

Later that night she thought about her strengths and wanted to be able to understand these for herself. She completed the VIA Character Strengths Survey, a free online scientific survey that defines top character strengths. It took just over ten minutes and revealed her key five strengths as:

1. **Humility:** letting one's accomplishments speak for themselves; not regarding oneself as more special than one is.
2. **Kindness:** doing favours and good deeds for others; helping them; taking care of them.
3. **Appreciation of Beauty and Excellence**: noticing and appreciating beauty, excellence, and/or skilled performance in various domains of life, from nature to art to mathematics to science to everyday experience.
4. **Prudence:** being careful about one's choices; not taking undue risks; not saying or doing things that might later be regretted.
5. **Perseverance:** finishing what one starts; persevering in a course of action despite obstacles; getting it out the door; taking pleasure in completing tasks.

As Carla reflected on the descriptors she smiled. No wonder: I put everyone else first, she thought. She also realised that being careful not to take risks might be part of the reason she didn't feel able to speak up in her appraisal. She had been in her corporate role for a long time and not progressed any further, not wanting to take any risks and push too far while the children were young. Maybe that's something I should ABC, she thought, it might well be time to challenge those beliefs.

The real showstopper for Carla was the strength of Appreciation of Beauty. When she and Pete were first together, they would spend hours at the local art exhibitions, admiring art in all its forms from pottery, to paintings, to glassblowing; they loved the detail, creativity, and the effort put into it. Their first date was such a special day: the afternoon at one of the big galleries in the city followed by tickets to a show. They had not done anything like that for years now; it was too much effort with the children, and finding time for themselves was way down the list of priorities.

She spoke to Pete about the survey and shared her strengths with him, reminding him too of the joy they used to share. "Why don't we find time for the things we love to do Pete?"

"Good question, but you know the answer, when would we have time? Who would watch the kids? Life just gets in the way."

"Do you think it would be fun for you to do the survey Pete? What do you think your top strengths would be?" Carla picked up the laptop. Fifteen minutes later, Pete shared his results:

1. **Teamwork:** Working well as a member of a group or team – being loyal to the group – doing one's share.
2. **Honesty:** Speaking the truth, but more broadly presenting oneself in a genuine and sincere way – being without pretence – taking responsibility for one's feelings and actions.
3. **Appreciation of Beauty and Excellence:** Noticing and appreciating beauty, excellence, and/or skilled performance in various domains of life, from nature to art to mathematics to science to everyday experience.
4. **Self-regulation:** Regulating what one feels and does – being disciplined – controlling one's appetites and emotions.
5. **Leadership:** Encouraging a group of which one is a member to get things done and at the same time maintain good relations within the group – organising group activities and seeing that they happen.

They looked at each other, smiling. "We share number three," they said together.

"Wouldn't it be something if the kids shared the strength too, what do you think?" Pete asked.

"I wouldn't be surprised if it was in there somewhere. Ella and Joe have both chosen art at school, and Lily loves watching ballet," Carla replied. "You know, these strengths can help us to live our best life. It's certainly helped me think about how I am at work. As well as reminding me how much we loved spending time appreciating the creativity of other people. Thinking about it the house is full of pictures, ceramics, pots and I have never been able to throw away a single picture that the kids drew."

"We should find those pictures, take a little trip down memory lane," Pete suggested.

"What a great idea. Can we also plan in a gallery day?" Carla asked.

Something to try

Complete the VIA Strengths to identify your top five to eight strengths at:
www.viacharacter.org/survey/account/register
It is completely free to use and the instructions for access are straightforward. When completing the survey, don't agonise over each statement; take the one that feels most like you.

The tool allows us to identify which of the strengths we have to a greater or lesser degree and provides some descriptors that give us the vocabulary to understand and use them. The fact they have been developed and applied to an extensive and ongoing scientific research project gives us confidence in them.

Once you have identified your top five strengths, start to be more aware of them over the next few weeks. For example:

- Notice when they are in play
- When they are helpful
- When they are in the way
- When they help you relax/recover/be yourself

Activity for the whole family

All members aged ten and above to complete VIA.

Then each, on a large piece of paper, draw them, represent them in some way, in a visual/illustrative way. Then share them. Each person has five minutes to share while everyone else listens. Also include a time when your strengths have helped and a time when they might have obstructed you.

Summary

All human beings have strengths that are valuable personally and to others. We have learnt that:

- There are twenty-four characteristics that human beings admire in each other.
- These have been set out in a helpful list, alongside a tool to help us identify our top five strengths.
- Our strengths take self-intelligence to understand and manage.
- They provide a scientific way to understand the best of ourselves.

A messy kind of magic   12
Achieving mastery of the skills

Prevention is better than cure, and education is better than prevention.

It's time now to bring together the eight skills that you have learned, one by one, chapter by chapter, just as you would learn, one element at a time, how to drive a car or speak a foreign language. Congratulations: you have achieved proficiency!

With those skills in place, we can consider how you can practise, use, and develop them, so they become truly just a part of you, how you think, feel, and behave. Then, you will have achieved mastery. To help you towards that goal, we will:

- Remind you of the individual skills and how and when to use them
- Explore the magic of the spiral effect, when skills can be woven together
- Imagine this: a final encounter with Carla and Pete and their family
- Spot the difference: notice how your teenagers are displaying the behaviours of psychological fitness

Remember this?

As you look at the graphic now, ask yourself:

- which skill do I like best?
- which skill do I find easiest?
- which skill do I need to study more?

DOI: 10.4324/9781003581994-13

Self-awareness skills					Superpower skills			
Skills To Harness Emotions	ABC	Reframing	Big Sticky Beliefs		WoBbLe	Moving On	Managing The Moment	Playing To Strengths
Understanding our emotions. Identifying if emotions are helpful or unhelpful. Techniques to harness emotions as a strategy.	The link between our thoughts, our feelings, and our behaviour.	Understanding habits in our thinking and how to create optimistic and realistic alternatives.	Identifying value-based beliefs and identifying when and how they influence us.		Managing catastrophic thinking	Creating new understandings of old problems. Avoiding the confirmation bias. Identifying new ways of moving forward	Using shortcut versions of all the skills to manage in the moment.	Identifying strengths. Making the most of our strengths. Recognising how they help and hinder us.

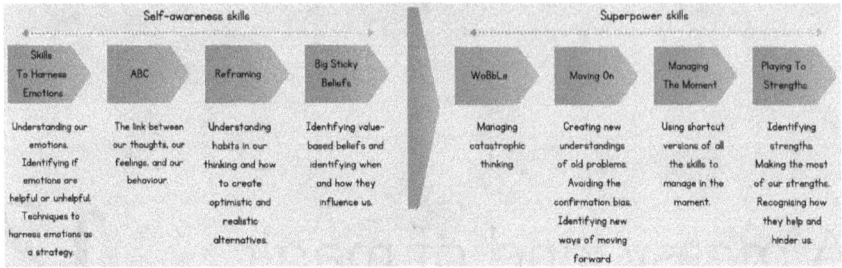

The listing of the following skills will help you identify when and how to use the eight elements of psychological fitness.

Self-awareness skills

Harnessing Emotions – use this skill:

- When you feel yourself filling up. Getting a bit agitated, annoyed. Do something that enables you to experience feeling calm and relaxed.
- During times when you are juggling a lot of competing demands, remember to put the oxygen mask on yourself. Take five minutes to recover.
- When you are stuck somewhere that you have no control over, use the time to breathe; focus on what you can be grateful for.

ABC – use this skill:

- In the moments when you feel a little knocked in some way and don't let the small things build up.
- When you react in a way that is unhelpful to you.
- When you want to understand the beliefs that are driving the way you are feeling and behaving.

Reframing – use this skill:

- In the small moments when you feel more than a little knocked and you want to decide what to do.
- When you react in a way that is unhelpful to you or to those around you.
- When something is playing on your mind because you didn't handle it the way you usually would.

Big Sticky Beliefs – use this skill:

- When you have overreacted to a situation.
- When there is a disconnect between how you feel and how you behave. For example, your beliefs are such that you should be feeling angry, but instead you feel guilty, and it doesn't make any sense to you.
- When you can't make your mind up. You have weighed up the options but still you can't decide what to do, for example to take the promotion that's great for your career but means you will be home much later.

Superpower skills

WoBbLe – use these skills:

- When you are thinking the worst, snowballing negative thoughts. For example: when you pick up a voice message from your teenager's head teacher; or your child is not picking up their phone; or your fifteen-year-old wants to go to a party that finishes late.
- When you are making a mountain out of a Himalaya or a Himalaya out of a mountain.

Moving On – use these skills:

- On a recurring situation that repeats and hasn't been resolved.
- When particular types of situations are a problem for you. For example, when you must speak in public, or confront someone in authority, or a certain person that always seems to rub you up the wrong way.
- When you say the same thing over and over and believe your teenager does not pay any attention to you.

Managing the Moment – use these skills:

- When you must do something, a presentation at work for example, and your mind starts to tell you that you can't do it.
- The first time you are faced with the situation you recently used ABC on.
- When you can feel your temperature rising.

Playing to Strengths – use these skills:

- To remind you who you are.
- When thinking about what recovery is for you, doing something that plays to your strengths.
- To dial down your strengths when you can see them getting in the way.
- When using your strengths to come at a problem in a different way.
- For job interviews, when meeting a new partner, with your children to model being proud of your uniqueness.

Pulling it all together with ease and grace comes with practice. Don't pressure yourselves; try to develop a daily habit of trying one of the skills, to maintain your understanding. When you're feeling confident, be more ambitious and challenge yourself to push yourself out of your comfort zone, into your stretch zone, to experiment a little. If it doesn't work, well, that's good learning, failing well!

The spiral effect

Whilst some adversities are relatively straightforward to work with, requiring only one skill to resolve, others can need more complicated responses. The weaving together of a few skills is called the spiral effect, and it's a kind of magic.

Here are some examples:

In Chapter 4, we see Carla and Ella at loggerheads because they had both forgotten to buy eggs for Ella's cookery class. The self-awareness ABC skill was really all that was needed to resolve the matter.

More involved situations may require a combination of a couple of skills. In Chapter 8, we see Ella catastrophising because she had not been invited to a friend's party. In this case Carla first used the self-awareness harnessing emotions skill to neutralise Ella's impending panic, before using the WoBbLe superpower skill to gain perspective.

Complicated situations that have built up over a period of time will use more than two skills. When Pete learns that Ella thinks Lily is his favourite, he is thrown into turmoil. With Carla's help, he completed several skills: first ABC, then reframing, and finally, with Carla's help to see what he might be missing to challenge his beliefs, the moving on skill.

Imagine this

Pete's dad, Brian, aged eighty-one, passed away after a short period of illness. It was a shock for Pete and the rest of the family, one of those big situations where the rug seemed to have been pulled out from beneath Pete's feet and floored him. He was close to his dad and could talk to him about most things; he valued his opinion, and he was devasted by his loss.

Carla lost her mum not long after having Joe, so she truly understood. She had deep empathy for Pete, knowing how much he relied on his dad's guidance. She was also deeply sad herself; she loved Brian too. He had been a rock when she was grieving the loss of her mum. He always seemed to know what to say, when to step in and help her out with Joe, and when to keep his distance.

Carla was also worried about Joe as he was close to his granddad, who had been a big part of his life from early on. He had a bond different to the girls.

Carla told Joe on his own, away from the girls and Pete's grief. She knew it would be one of the most difficult conversations she would have with her son so far. She thought about when and where would be best, so that beforehand she could act intentionally to make time for herself to recover. She took to her journal and wrote words almost unconsciously, jotting down her concerns, what she didn't want to say, or have happen. She wrote about how she was feeling and her predictions for the way Joe would react.

Writing like this allowed her to release some of the anxiety she was feeling but also allowed her to look at her thoughts and feelings with more objectivity. Words seemed to jump out of the page, and she could reframe the most unhelpful thoughts.

In the half an hour before she planned to talk to Joe, she did some breath work to recover her racing brain. She focused on how grateful she was that Brian had been such a positive role model for Joe, and a wonderful father-in-law.

She went into the conversation with Joe ready emotionally, feeling confident in her ability to comfort him, to say the right things, to allow him to express his emotions in whatever form they came.

Afterwards they both did a simple breathing exercise together, holding hands.

Carla asked Joe, "What would Gramps say to us if he was here now?"

"He'd probably be staring at us strangely and be asking what on earth we were doing," Joe said.

Carla laughed. "He would, what mumbo jumbo he would say, right?"

"It does help though mum, even though I feel a bit of a twat doing it," Joe said.

"It gets easier with time, and when something so devasting happens we need little ways to look after ourselves. Your dad needs us and we need each other." Carla put her arm around Joe and pulled him close.

"Grampa always knew the right thing to say, I never felt judged by him, he made me feel calm and peaceful," Joe said.

"He would feel so proud that you are telling me that Joe. That's a legacy you can take with you of him for always. Find others to share what he taught you, that way you keep him with you."

They took a moment together, held each other tight.

Later that day when Pete came back, he looked ashen. Carla tried to greet him with a hug, but he pulled away. "Not now Carla, I need to be on my own."

This went on for some weeks. Each time Carla tried to talk to Pete or show him any affection he rejected her. Carla understood but it didn't make it any easier. Some days she let it go, others she would make a comment. "You are going to have to let me in soon," she would say, only to be ignored again.

The funeral came and went. It was a busy time, keeping the house going, supporting the children, talking to the school, balancing work. Life had to go on. Carla was feeling the pressure. She was writing more and more in her journal, practising her daily recovery, ABCing the life out of situations, and reframing her thoughts to be as optimistic and realistic as possible, but she needed Pete to let her in.

Pete and Carla shared the strength of appreciation of beauty and excellence, and she decided this could be a way to open up lines of communication between them.

> *Appreciation of Beauty and Excellence: Noticing and appreciating beauty, excellence, and/or skilled performance in various domains of life, from nature to art to mathematics to science to everyday experience.*

She called Pete's work, something she would never normally do, but she felt sure that they would be worried about him. She spoke to his PA Siobhan and asked her to suggest a date that would be ok for Pete to take off. Siobhan was glad she had called as she was so worried about him. "I've never seen him like this Carla, I wanted to call you, but he told me how sad you and the kids were, so I didn't want to burden you."

Carla felt such a sense of relief he was at least talking to Siobhan about how Brian's passing was affecting them all. They decided on a Tuesday to give some time for Carla to tell Pete.

Carla booked the day off work herself and arranged for the kids to go to her neighbour after school. That night she told Pete about the plans in as calm and clear a way as she could:

"Look darling, it's been a few months now since your dad passed and we have not yet had time to talk about it. When we don't talk, I feel less able to cope with everything. I feel like you are shutting me out. I want to help, and

I need you. I have made plans and arranged for us to go out for the day to the local art gallery. I have sorted it with Siobhan, and she has cleared your work diary. I would really like it if you just said yes. I have thought hard about it; I think it would help you and it would be helpful for me. What do you think?"

Pete looked at her, his eyes filling up. "I am so sorry love, I feel so empty and hollow right now. I just can't go out where there will be people we know, but I would like to spend some time with you." They reached for each other and hugged for the first time since Brian's death.

Rather than going out, they agreed to do some art at home. Carla unrolled a large piece of paper and lots of colouring pens, art stuff, and suggested they draw out their feelings about Brian. They talked about him, Pete shared some early memories, they cried lots. Carla drew Brian as a guardian for her and Joe and shared something she had never told Pete about her relationship with his dad. They cried some more. They hugged and felt close.

As the afternoon moved into early evening and Carla knew the children would be home soon, she asked, "Shall we share this with them?"

Pete thought it was a great idea. "Not tonight though eh!"

"Agreed," said Carla, "I would like to explain to them how we have spent the day though and tell them we want to share it with them soon."

"I would like that," Pete said, "the weekend would be good."

"Maybe we could do something similar together, if they would be up for it. A picture of all the things we are grateful about Gramps," she said, and Pete agreed.

At the weekend they came together as a family to express their gratitude for Grandpa Brian. It wasn't the last time they cried or felt his loss; they would never be the same again, but it was the beginning of the healing process of grief. It was a way to express their feelings together as family, possibly because they had self-efficacy and their self-belief; they had skills that helped them find a way through.

Life is tough and getting it right all the time is impossible. Being psychologically fit is often about doing things well enough. It's also about reaching out for help when needed. Resilience is not about dealing with everything and keeping going, and it is not a one-size-fits-all approach.

Spot the difference: the behaviours of psychological fitness

Our hope, in these closing pages, is that you will be able to recognise the developing skills of your teenagers, to notice when they are using them well; catch them doing something right, as the saying goes. Then you can offer praise and encouragement that will nurture their growth and support the development of their psychological fitness.

There are five key behaviours that you can look out for. Spotting them is the best way to measure the differences in your teenager's behaviour.

Flexible and realistic thinking: you see them being curious and open to different perspectives. They can look for evidence to solve problems effectively, seek help, and ask questions to explore solutions. They are wedded to reality, meaning they are grounded in their real life, not exaggerating or minimising what is going on.

When you see and hear these behaviours, use process praise to encourage more of the same. For example:

- It was smart to ask a few different people how they would deal with that.
- You are open to different ideas; that is such a strength.
- You are good at finding solutions. Can you use your detective skills and help me see what I am missing here?
- It was brave to notice things are tough at school right now, and that you needed some support.

Self-awareness and compassion: They can explain and/or show an understanding of themselves by expressing how and why they reacted as they did. They know what is normal or usual for them and are therefore able to ask for help when needed. They show and express kindness and compassion for themselves and to others.

When you see and hear these behaviours, use process praise to encourage more of the same. For example:

- The way you described what happened and how that felt was impressive.
- I could see you were anxious, but in control of it, so a normal reaction; do you agree?
- I felt so proud of the compassion you showed Joe when his pet died, being there to comfort him and look out for him.

Human connection: They are connected to other people in a variety of ways, at home, at school, in the community. They are willing to reach out to people, to make new friends. They have empathy and care for others knowing that will increase personal happiness.

When you see and hear these behaviours, use process praise to encourage more of the same. For example:

- You have such a wide mix of friends. It's great you have friends you grew up with, go to school with, and who live nearby.
- Amelia was telling me how kind you were to her. What happened? Tell me.
- So that is three new people you have met in a couple of days; you are on a roll, love that!

Hope and optimism: They set realistic goals and believe that they can reach them. They think optimistically, are focused and upbeat about themselves and the world around them.

When you see and hear these behaviours use process praise to encourage more of the same. For example:

- It is hard sometimes to set ourselves goals; you make me so proud you have personal targets. Let me know if I can help.
- I'm glad to hear you choosing the optimistic way of seeing that. It would have been easier to be pessimistic and look, now you have achieved it.
- It fills my heart with joy when I see you thinking ahead with options and confidence in yourself.

Self-regulation: They understand the impact and range of emotions people can feel. They can control their impulses, by spending time being calm and focused.

When you see and hear these behaviours, use process praise to encourage more of the same. For example:

- When you walked away from your sister, I could see you counting to ten. Well done you, such a superpower!
- I feel proud that you have worked hard saving up for that new game. It can't have been easy when I know some of your friends got theirs before you. Good things come to those who wait.
- I didn't want to interrupt you earlier, but can you show me that breathing exercise I saw you doing? I need to take more time to recover the way you do.

Training yourself to focus on noticing what's going well is a great discipline, and an antidote to our habit of noticing what's wrong. Catch someone doing something right! Make it a daily habit to boost your children's confidence by process praising them about the good things you noticed.

Summary

Learning how to apply the skills, where and when, is one of the routes to mastery. And learning how to spot the changing behaviour of your teenagers and offering them appropriate process praise will motivate you to keep learning and developing your own skills. We have learnt that:

- Each skill can be used on their own, or in combinations. How and when to use them will depend on the situation, and the scale of the problem.
- The magic of the spiral effect is when skills can be woven together.
- Applying the skills to the big situations, such as losing a close relative, is when self-efficacy is present.
- Look out for your teenagers displaying the behaviours of psychological fitness and use process praise to encourage and grow their capacity.

Reflections on the future of parenting 13

We should create as much happiness and the least misery for ourselves and those around us.

Today's parents do not receive the credit they deserve. We would go as far to say you are the lost generation of parents, raising your teenagers in a rapidly changing world, without the wisdom of elders. You are walking on the bridge while you are building it. Now that you have studied psychological fitness, you have the knowledge to teach your teenagers well, using the skills as your guide.

You are the ambassadors for our future generations of parents.

Balancing the analogue and digital worlds

The future of parenting is undeniably about the advances of digital technologies, which have happened at lightning speed. Information technology is integrated into our everyday lives and our teenagers do not know a world without information literally at their fingertips. The way we engage with media, including social media platforms, is evolving rapidly and it's important that we engage and teach young people in the context of their lived experience.

The counterpoint to digital overload is to remember and promote the simple wholesome elements of the analogue world: walking in the woods or by the sea, playing games in the garden, doing jigsaws, painting pictures, cooking interesting meals, eating together, telling jokes, laughing,

DOI: 10.4324/9781003581994-14

conversations and discussions of interesting topics. These generate such a different energy from the fast-moving digital world, people sitting as still as statues in front of multiple screens, watching a stream of soundbites and complex data.

Education is better than prevention

We've said this before, and we'll say it again:

> *When it comes to mental health, prevention is better than cure, and education is better than prevention.*

It is our dearest hope that the future of parenting will be for the provision of psychological education for teenagers to become a natural part of the school curriculum. We cannot stress enough the importance of teaching teenagers these preventative skills. Not only does this tried and tested method protect them against mental health problems, but it also offers the opportunity to thrive and flourish, to live life in a way that is in the best interest of human-kind: not chasing our tails for unreachable perfection but being present and living our lives in the best way we can.

Mastering the skills

It's easy to understand the skills when reading off the page, but putting them routinely into practice takes time. Don't expect superpowers too soon, for yourself or your children. Remember, failure is a learning opportunity. This is a new skill set, a new language. Go back over some of the worksheets and exercises. Practice makes perfect. Well, better, anyway.

We wish you kindness, health, love, happiness, and joy as you continue to develop your own skills for the sake of your family's well-being, and to make the world a better, happier, thriving place.

Books for children

We believe that books are a thing of wonder. Available to borrow from libraries or free in pop-up book recycling booths. Encouraging your off-spring to read is a gift for life.

There is an array of books for children that help explain everything about the world around them. You know your children best and so we recommend you do your own research, talk to friends and family, and their school about specific books.

Kids' books are usually a great read for adults too, and this is the best way to know whether it will be something they might like. Why not start a family book club and choose a book that you all read and discuss?

Here are some ideas:

- Social media:
  - *How to Break Up With Your Phone* by Catherine Price
  - *Your Mind Matters* by Honor Head
- The planet:
  - *Eyes Wide Open* by Paul Fleischman
  - *Heart to Heart* by His Holiness the Dalai Lama
- Relationships:
  - *You Don't Understand Me* by Dr Tara Porter
  - *Impossible Creatures* by Katherine Rundell
- Resilience:
  - *When Stars Are Scattered* by Victoria Jamieson and Omar Mohamed
  - *You Are Awesome* by Matthew Syed
- Loss:
  - *You Will Be Okay* by Julie Stokes
  - *Hope Is Our Only Wing* by Rutendo Tavengerwei

Suggested reading for adults

There are so many books that have influenced us over the years in this space. Here are some suggestions for additional reading.

Clarke, A., Fleche, S., Layard. R., Powdthavee, N., Ward, G. (2019). *The Origins of Happiness: The science of well-being over the life course.* Princeton University Press.

Coleman, J. (2021). *The Teacher and the Teenage Brain.* Routledge.

Dolan, P. (2015). *Happiness By Design: Finding pleasure and purpose in everyday life.* The Penguin Group.

Dweck, C. (2007). *Mindset: The new psychology of success.* Ballantine Books.

Fredrickson, B. (2009). *Positivity: Groundbreaking Research Reveals How to Embrace the Hidden Strength of Positive Emotions, Overcome Negativity, and Thrive.* Crown Archetype.

Grace Lordan, G. (2021). *Think Big.* Penguin.

Layard, R. (2020). *Can We Be Happier? Evidence and ethics.* Pelican.

Lyubomirsky, S. (2007).*The How of Happiness: A practical guide to getting the life you want.* Penguin.

Murthy, V. (2020). *Together: The Healing Power of Human Connection in a Sometimes Lonely World*. Harper Collins Publishers.

Obama, M. (2022). *The Light We Carry: Overcoming in uncertain times*. Random House Group.

Seligiman, M. (2012). *Flourish: A New Understanding of Happiness and Wellbeing*. Simon & Schuster.

Vaillant, G. (2003). *Ageing Well: Surprising Guideposts to a Happier Life from the Landmark Harvard Study of Adult Development*. Little, Brown & Company.

Williams, M., Penman, D. (2011). *Mindfulness: Finding Peace in a Frantic World*. Piatkus Books.

Index

For Product Safety Concerns and Information please contact our EU
representative GPSR@taylorandfrancis.com
Taylor & Francis Verlag GmbH, Kaufingerstraße 24, 80331 München, Germany